Gardeners Not Mechanics

How to Cultivate Change at Work

Gary Lloyd

For my wonderful wife Doris, for her enthusiasm and support, without which I would not have persisted.

CONTENTS

'Life's not about finding yourself; life's about creating yourself.'

Bob Dylan

Introduction

Sustainable change is elusive. Whether it's as significant as Brexit or as personal as finding a job you love, the obstacles are surprisingly similar. Perhaps more surprisingly, the solutions are also similar. This book covers both of these types of change and it has one big idea that links them together.

The world of work is an ecosystem of interdependent organisations, groups and individuals.

If you want to make a sustainable change at work, you are more likely to succeed if you approach your change as a gardener, not a mechanic.

Mechanics rely on predictability. They assume that the same inputs produce the same outputs, time after time. A car, for example, will perform as predicted on a tarmac road. Put it in a ploughed field, however, and its performance will be unpredictable. Machines need well-defined, controlled environments in which to perform well.

In contrast, gardeners know that their environment is unpredictable, with much of it outside their control. So, gardeners take small steps towards a bigger goal. They experiment in order to find out what works and what doesn't, and continually adjust to what they find out. They know there is no guarantee that what worked before will work again, because they know their environment is in a constant state of flux.

China's one-child policy, introduced in 1980, is an example of what can happen when you approach change as a mechanic. In the 1970s, the Chinese government became concerned that it would be unable to sustain its expanding population. It convened an all-male group of cyberneticists and engineers to address the problem. The group concluded that China's ideal population would be 700 million and that the way to achieve this was to limit births.[1]

Forty years after the introduction of the policy, China is facing a demographic time-bomb. Currently 12% of China's population is over 60. By 2050, it will rise to 34%. Deutsche Bank calculates a pension shortfall of trillions of dollars.

Also, many men have difficulty finding partners with whom to have children because the population has become skewed towards males. You don't have to think too hard about this to understand a terrible side-effect of the policy. Unforeseen, often unwanted side-effects are a characteristic of ecosystems.

And now, even though the restrictions have now been loosened, many families are still only having one child. Mei Fong, author of *One Child: The Story of China's Most Radical Experiment*[2], says:

> '*The whole policy was drafted by missile scientists. It*
> *was based around mechanical systems, where you*

set a target then adjust accordingly. Women's bodies were treated like engines; you set inputs and expect to get a certain output.

The architect of the whole (one-child) project acknowledged many years ago that an ageing population could eventually lead to problems, but just said "that can be adjusted". As if women's bodies can just be treated like levers, moved up and down.'

Regrettably, the government didn't see fit to involve social scientists, who would have approached the challenge more like gardeners. Those "gardeners" would have understood that the context for change was an unpredictable system of relationships and human behaviour. And they would have understood the need to monitor the effects of any changes continually because social systems often evolve in unexpected ways when exposed to change.

But you don't need to be a social scientist or get bogged down in systems theory to avoid thinking mechanistically. As I'll illustrate in this book, the analogy of gardening will take you down those same paths, without getting embroiled in jargon or theory.

The examples I use in this book are a mix of organisational and personal change. But actually, they are two sides of the same coin. Too often, we see change as something we do to others. We use phrases such as getting buy-in. We forget at our peril that change usually depends as much on a shift in our own assumptions, beliefs and behaviours, as it does on those of others.

This is well understood by Justine Roberts, founder of *Mumsnet*. In an interview for the BBC podcast 'The Disrupters'[3], she was asked about the challenges of scaling up her business. She said:

> *'It came home to me when a really good member of the team tweeted something from our Mumsnet account that was a total anathema to what I thought were the values of Mumsnet. And I thought, how did that happen, it was clearly my fault, right? I hadn't communicated that, so I'm going to have to work out how I change my job to deal with that.'*

The idea for the book originated with a workshop I ran for client's *emerging leaders forum*. As part of the workshop I asked each participant to focus on a challenge they had in their workplace. During a plenary session, one of the participants asked me how I would approach something with which she had been struggling. In general, I try to avoid giving direct advice, because it's more effective when people develop their own solutions.

My brain was urging me to say her problem would benefit from an approach that combined aspects of behavioural science, design thinking, lean thinking and systems thinking. But I knew I couldn't use those terms without putting everyone to sleep and losing their attention for the rest of the day. Instead, I froze and started to sweat slightly as the silent room looked to me for inspiration.

Then I heard myself saying, "try thinking and acting like a gardener, not a mechanic". She looked at me, quizzically. But before I could explain, the other participants started to chip in, with ideas about what it would

4

mean to be a gardener in her situation. It was a facilitator's dream. The room took a straightforward analogy and used it as a tool to generate and explore novel ideas and pathways that encompassed all of the jargon-laden topics I had in mind, but free of the jargon or theory.

I mentioned the "incident" to my wife when I called home that evening. "You're on to something," she said. "Think about how it applies to personal development? What does it mean to cultivate a skill or nurture an individual?" Then she, like my participants, was off and running with examples.

Over the next couple of years, I wove the phrase, *gardeners not mechanics* into my work with consultancy and coaching clients. I would ask what the analogy meant to them, in their context. It enabled us all to think and talk in ecosystem terms, but using something familiar.

The book is divided into two parts. Part I describes the key ideas, including a description of three core characteristics of ecosystems:

- Unpredictability
- Interdependence
- Limits of control

Unpredictability is often the product of the other two, but not always, especially when it comes to human behaviour, which is inherently unpredictable, as we shall see. And anyway, if you were to focus solely on the latter two in the above list, you might be seduced by the notion that you can create an accurate predictive model, like a mechanic.

Beware, however, of what Mervyn King, the former Governor of the Bank of England, calls 'bogus quantification'[4]. King was running the UK's central bank during the 2008 financial crisis. In a talk given at the London School of Economics, he tells how the UK bank Northern Rock proposed, at its 2007 Annual General Meeting, to give money back to shareholders, because it didn't need it.

But 'weeks later, they literally ran out of money'. King said that Northern Rock had used the *risk weights* devised in Basel by central bankers and regulators, but these weights gave a false sense of security that completely ignored *sentiment*.

Going on to talk about what he calls *radical uncertainty*[5], he said that 'you can't put all of your eggs in one basket. You need a variety of responses that keep your options open'. To which I would add: just like a gardener, planting different crops of vegetables in different places.

The second part of the book illustrates how you can think like a gardener when you want to make a change at work. It uses a framework entitled 'The Elements of Gardening' borrowed from the late Christopher Lloyd[6], the legendary English gardener. Each element is an analogy you can use to direct your thinking down paths that might otherwise remain unexplored.

There is one chapter for each of Lloyd's nine elements of gardening:

- Plan
- Prepare the soil
- Plant
- Prune
- Weed

- Water
- Stake
- Ensure good health
- Enjoy your harvest

The purpose of these chapters is not to tell you how you should think or what tools you should use. Instead, I aim to stimulate your creativity by sharing examples and 'gardening tools' I have found useful in my work.

However, you will get most from the analogy given in the title of the chapter if you pick it up and run with it yourself, inspired by the examples and tools in this book.

To help you along the way, there are exercises throughout the book to prompt you to think about a real change you want to make. If you do these exercises, you will gain two benefits. First, you will have practised thinking like a gardener, using a real example you can relate to. Second, you will think deeply about how to achieve a change that is important to you.

I'll start the first part of the book by diving straight into an organisational change story – one that illustrates the difference between a gardener and a mechanic. You may not find yourself faced with a challenge of the magnitude described, but the same principles apply to changes of any size or type, as are the other examples I have used in this book.

Part I

Key Ideas

Machine or Ecosystem?

A Mechanical Failure

On the day that *J.C. Penney* announced Ron Johnson as its new Chief Executive Officer (CEO), its stock price rose by 17%. Penney board member Bill Ackman, whose hedge fund owned 18% of J.C. Penny, described Johnson as 'the Steve Jobs of retailing'[7].

By the time Johnson took up his post at the struggling department store chain in November 2011, optimism had pushed the stock price up by nearly 50%, from $24 to $35. After announcing his vision and strategy in January 2012, the stock price climbed even further to $42.

Eighteen months after he took up his post, the J.C. Penney Board fired Johnson, with the stock price at $16. Bill Ackman said that Johnson's reign was 'very close to a disaster'.

Up until then, Johnson had a stellar career in retailing, first at 'superstore' retailer *Target* and then at *Apple*.

A graduate of Stanford University and Harvard Business School, Johnson started his retailing career at Mervyn's, a California-based retailer, with nearly 200 stores in 10 states.

'I wanted to run a company one day', said Johnson, 'and I needed to learn the business from the ground up. I took a job in the stockroom, and I figured if I worked hard, put my head down, I would work my way up to have a chance to lead.'

After he joined Target, it took him 10 years, from 1990 to 2000, to work his way up from the head of housewares to vice-president of merchandising. His big idea was to introduce designer wares into Target stores. It worked. Target gained a reputation as a hip place to shop and increased its number of stores by about 50% during Johnson's tenure, from 600 to 900, in 40 states.

In 2000, Steve Jobs recruited Johnson to create Apple's retail stores. Up until then, Apple sold through other retailers, such as Target, but Jobs felt that this didn't give Apple sufficient control over showing Apple products in their best light. By 2011, Apple had 300 stores worldwide and was ranked first in the US for dollar sales per square foot.

After he joined J.C. Penny, Johnson moved quickly. In late January 2012, he announced a three- part plan:

- Eliminate discount pricing.
- Organise merchandise by brand, not function.
- Rebrand as JCP.

His vision was a store with individual brand boutiques, shops within a shop. The boutiques would be organised around a 'town centre' where customers could meet, eat and interact with friends. A J.C. Penney store would become a destination, not just a place to shop. He got rid of cash registers, replacing them with roaming employees, checking out customers using iPads, just as was done at Apple.

Over the following 12 months, Johnson rolled out his vision to 1,100 stores. Challenged over the risk of his approach, he said: 'at Apple, we didn't test anything'.

In actual fact, at both Target and Apple, Johnson had indeed "tested everything" before rolling out changes. At Target, he conducted small-scale experiments, gradually introducing designer products and gauging reaction.

And Apple didn't have a single store when Johnson arrived. He created mock-ups in a warehouse near Apple's headquarters to test out ideas. Then Apple began with just two stores. Every new store opening after that was effectively an experiment. Testing is in the DNA of most successful tech company, including the mighty Apple.

Johnson's contention that 'at Apple, we didn't test anything' sounds like the defensive response of a man in a hurry. Unfortunately for Johnson, however, J.C. Penney's existing customers were confused by the changes to the store layout and pricing. In particular, according to Corey Phelps, a strategy professor at McGill University, Penney's customers 'loved the thrill of hunting for the discounts', something that disappeared in the new format[8].

Already-falling sales plunged dramatically, along with a commensurate fall in the company share price. J.C. Penney's Board fired Johnson and replaced him with his predecessor, Mike Ullman, who undid almost every one of Johnson's changes.

According to Corey Phelps, Johnson had fallen into the common trap of assuming that what worked somewhere else would work in a new setting.

That, however, is not quite the end of the story. J.C. Penney continued to struggle after Johnson's departure. And three years after leaving J.C. Penny, Johnson told a retail conference in Las Vegas that the failure at J.C. Penney was due to the company's 'stagnant culture' and that 'people there were entrenched and resisting him.' He was unrepentant about his time at J.C. Penney, 'I still think if we had continued on, the company would have been a lot better than [that] painful U-turn', said Johnson.

In January 2019, *The Motley Fool* investment website wrote[9]:

> *'Johnson was on to something that is only now becoming apparent. Had he rolled out the changes in test markets to give customers time to acclimate to his new ideas, instead of launching them nationally all at once, he'd have had time to see which were more appropriate for the store and which were maybe too radical. Now, his ideas are being tested by other retailers who are being lauded as innovators.'*

Sadly, this is a familiar organisational change story. Someone who made a big splash in one place is appointed to a new, more senior or more prestigious role, determined to make a significant, fast, impact. The new appointee attributes their previous successes solely to their insight and determination, rather than circumstances in which they found themselves, the people that helped them or the organisational culture.

Psychologists call this phenomenon *the fundamental attribution error.* When we succeed, we tend to attribute our successes to our personal qualities and skills. When we fail, however, we tend to blame

14

unfavourable circumstances or other people. When we evaluate others, it's flipped. Others fail because they were not up to the task or succeed because they got lucky. It's evolutions default setting of all of us.

You can protect yourself against this sort of overconfidence by taking small steps, experimenting like a gardener, just like Johnson did at Target and Apple. A gardening approach doesn't preclude you from making significant organisational changes. The incremental changes Johnson made at Target and Apple accumulated into something that was industry-changing in both cases.

On the face of it, this story about J.C. Penney is about a failed organisational change. However, it's also a personal change story.

Johnson graduated in economics from Stanford, a university synonymous with Silicon Valley. He then did an MBA (Master of Business Administration) at the world's leading business school, Harvard. He turned down lucrative offers from investment banks and the lure of exciting technology start-ups. Instead, he pursued his passion for retailing, constructing his learning journey and experimenting with innovation whenever he got the chance.

When Johnson joined Apple in 2000, it wasn't the dominant player it is today. It had narrowly avoided bankruptcy a couple of years earlier and was still very much a niche player. Johnson felt, however, that the opportunity to work with Steve Jobs was simply too good miss.

When he left Apple for J.C. Penney in October 2010, Johnson left behind $50 million of stock options in what was, by then, one of the world's most profitable companies. Had he been solely interested in money, he would have stayed at Apple. He felt that Apple retail had reached a steady state and that there wasn't much challenge for him there.

He did receive compensatory stock options of $50 million from J.C. Penny, but these would only be available six years after joining and then only if the company performed well. He was so confident that he invested $50 million of his own money to buy more options at what he considered to be a favourable price. However, if the company underperformed, he stood to lose all of the options, including the $50 million of his own money.

It's clear that Johnson was not averse to taking risks. At Target and Apple, however, he took relatively small, calculated risks. In particular, he had a *growth mindset*, something I'll talk about in the chapter 'Ensure Good Health'. However, when he realised his stated ambition at J.C. Penney, which was 'to run a company one day', he seemed to forget that he might also need to change and to adapt to his new environment.

Some psychologists argue that our identities are made up of the stories we tell about ourselves. It's how we make sense of our experiences. Often our stories are about overcoming an obstacle and what we learned. But we can also become trapped by the narratives we create.

Perhaps Johnson became a prisoner of his own heroic story – someone who arrived at the pinnacle of retailing, through a journey of sacrifice and self-education, in the service of other people's visions. Maybe now was the time to bend the world to his viewpoint, not bend his viewpoint to the world?

It might not be your ambition 'to run a company one day', but you can still learn lessons from Johnson's story. Organisational and personal change are intertwined. The singer and songwriter Bob Dylan said[10]:

'Life isn't about finding yourself. Life is about creating yourself.'

A Poor Track Record

Just how typical, and how relevant, is J.C. Penney's failed change project? Towards the end of 2015, one of my clients asked me to run a *change leadership* workshop. I decided to start the workshop by asking participants to define the problem we were aiming to solve – in other words, why do we need a change leadership workshop in the first place?

As part of the discussion, I wanted to demonstrate that, in general, organisational change projects have a poor track record. I knew that the received wisdom, from numerous articles and books, was that 70% of change projects fail. I was keen to quote this dismal statistic of failure, but didn't want to do so without knowing where it came from.

However, the 70% figure turns out to be a bit of a myth. As I'll explain in the next section, a few influential authors in the mid-1990s expressed the 70% failure rate as an opinion, not the result of objective research. The figure is, however, frequently quoted in learned journals and books.

As I dug into the myth, I learned two things. First, it has become established as fact because it is credible. Suggest to someone you know that 70% of organisational change projects end in failure and they will probably respond with 'sounds about right'. It chimes with most people's experience of change projects.

The second thing I learned was that, for the last 20 years, management consultancies have used the myth to sell their shrink-wrapped recipes for change – recipes oriented towards top-down, big-bet projects that assume a world that is pretty much predictable.

If you agree with me that the environments in which we live and work are inherently unpredictable, you'll understand why those recipes have contributed to the poor performance of change projects, especially as one of those recipes has become the de facto standard for 'change management'.

Before I get to that, I want to tell you about my own research in order to try to find out whether the performance of change projects is as bad as everyone seems to think.

I asked 159 executive-level managers about their experience of change projects. I don't believe the binary choice between success or failure is helpful when looking at projects. Some projects don't deliver all of their expected value, but do, nonetheless, deliver some value. Is that a failure or a success?

So, instead of asking about failure, I asked the following question: how much of the expected value was delivered by projects of which you have direct personal knowledge?

As you can see from the results below, three-quarters of people reported that projects delivered 60% or less of the expected value. Two-thirds of people reported that half or less of the expected value was delivered. That's a pretty awful track record.

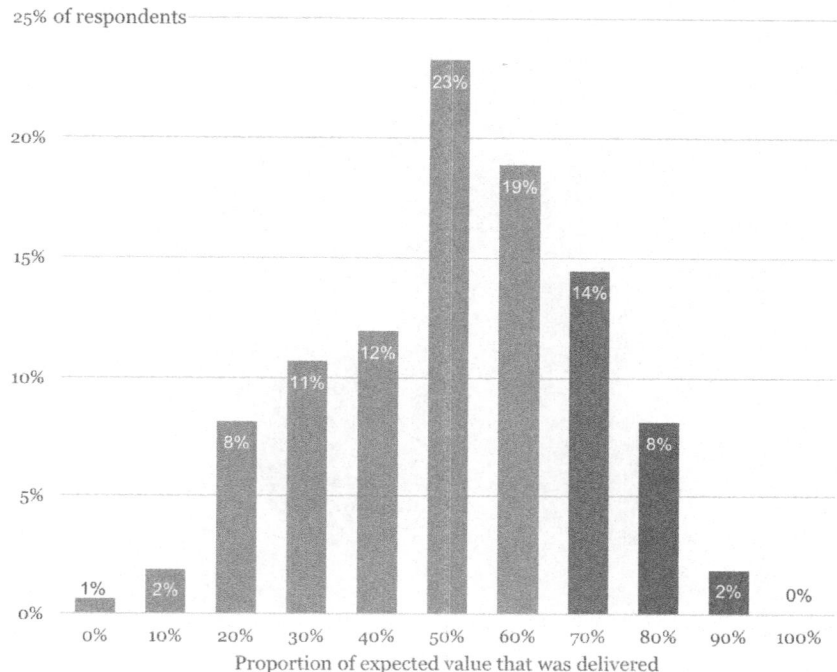

Next, I asked: 'What is the biggest mistake that organisations make?' I then looked at the frequency a mistake was mentioned and created the series of bubbles that you see below to reflect that frequency.

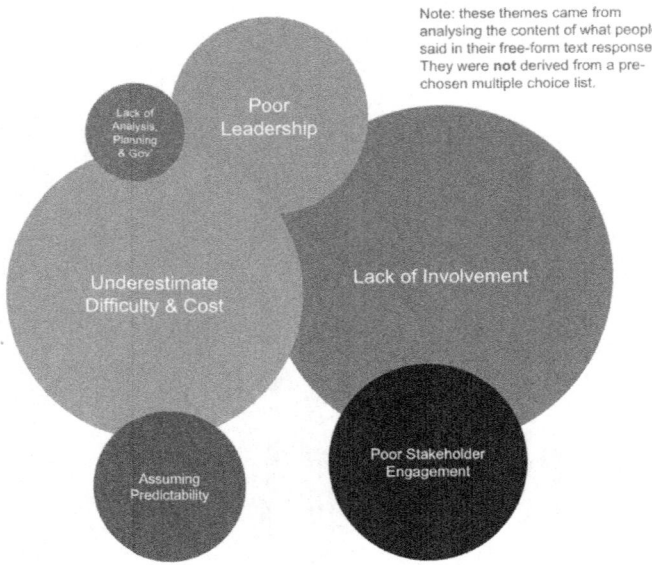

Note: these themes came from analysing the content of what people said in their free-form text responses. They were **not** derived from a pre-chosen multiple choice list.

Lack of Analysis, Planning & Gov'

Poor Leadership

Underestimate Difficulty & Cost

Lack of Involvement

Assuming Predictability

Poor Stakeholder Engagement

In an article I wrote for the professional body that supported the research, I summarised the consensus as follows[11]:

> *Most people thought that the value expected from change projects is usually overestimated and that difficulty is generally underestimated. The predominant approach was one of over-optimistic, big-bet, top-down projects that either press on with an inflexible Plan A, regardless of lack of measurable progress, or they run out of steam and willpower.*

Finally, I asked whether they thought that organisations are more like machines or ecosystems and whether they thought that organisations ran their change projects as if their organisations were machines or ecosystems:

- 72% of people said that organisations are more like ecosystems than machines.
- 90% said that organisations plan and execute change as if they were machines.

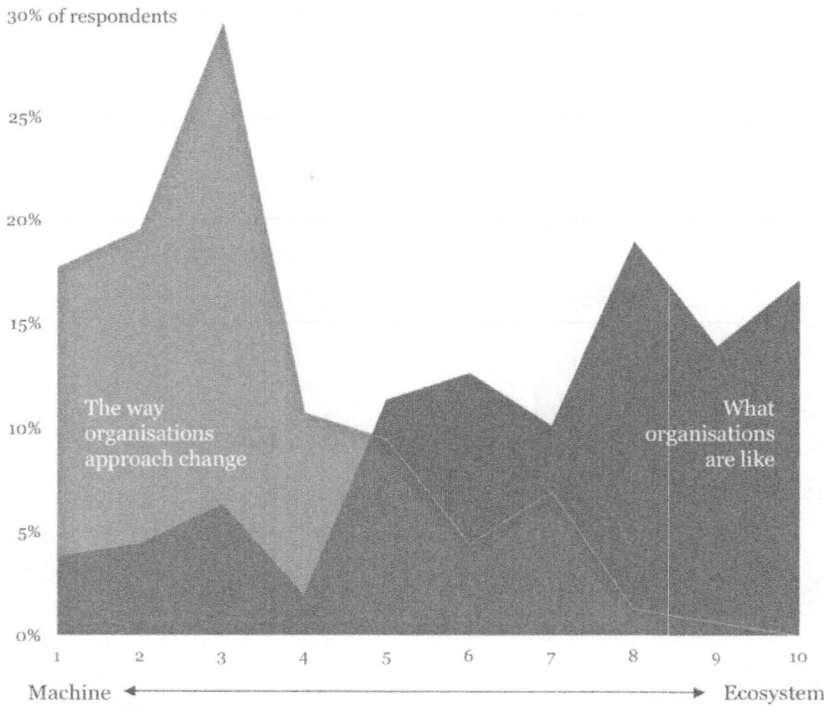

It's impossible to establish direct cause and effect, but when you look at the mistakes cited, it's clear that these equate to treating organisations as machines. It's also clear that the disparity between the way seasoned professionals see organisations (as ecosystems) and the way they see approaches to change (as machines) must have consequences for the value delivered by change projects.

Now, I know this is as much opinion based as the origin of the 70% myth, but I have not been able to find any research that evaluated the actual performance of 'change' projects as such. There has, however, been a lot of research into the performance of IT projects. If you accept that IT projects are usually enablers for large change projects, then we do have a lot of objective measures of performance, across thousands of projects worldwide.

The key findings of this research, described in Appendix A, are consistent with my own research.

Most projects underperform due to a range of behavioural, not technical, reasons.

The findings also highlight that the bigger the project, the more likely it is to fall short of expectations or not deliver at all.

The Big-Bet Death Grip

It's little wonder that the 70% failure rate remains plausible. It's probably not that wide of the mark, depending on how you define failure. However, it's impossible to separate its glibness from its origin, the industry and the mindset persists to this day.

In 1993 James Champy and Michael Hammer wrote an influential book entitled *Reengineering the Corporation: A Manifesto for Business*

Revolution[12]. It sold 2.5 million copies and was on the *New York Times* bestseller list for more than a year. At the time of publication, Hammer was a computer science professor at Massachusetts Institute of Technology (MIT), and Champy was a founder of Index, a $200 million management consulting practice, with a strong orientation towards technology-enabled change projects.

The book popularised the concept of *business process reengineering*. The authors' definition of reengineering is the epitome of a big-bang, the organisation as a machine approach. According to the authors, reengineering is defined by four keywords:

- Fundamental
- Radical
- Dramatic
- Processes

It's telling that these four keywords don't include 'people'. Reengineering is done to the people affected, not in collaboration with those affected. The drivers of change in this model are the 'leader, the process owner and the reengineering team'. A 'steering committee and a reengineering Czar' guide and oversee the change. The people are cogs in the machine who come with brains attached. Champy and Hammer write that:

> *'People need some reason to perform well within the reengineered process. It isn't enough to simply put new processes in place; managers must motivate employees to rise to the challenge of these processes by supporting the new values and beliefs the*

processes demanded. In other words, management
must pay attention to what goes on in people's heads
as well as what happens on their desks.'

The book's battle cry of 'reengineer of die' was soon adopted as a sales pitch by management consultancies that had large technology practices. When you put together a chapter entitled 'The Enabling Role of Information Technology' and words like 'fundamental', 'radical' and 'dramatic', you know you are going to have to spend a lot of money on IT.

Those same management consultancies also came equipped with a sure-fire recipe for reengineering success. 'Don't be one of the 70% of reengineering projects that fail', they told clients, drawing their scary statistic from Champy and Hammer.

What Champy and Hammer actually wrote was:

'Our unscientific estimate is that as many as 50% to
70% of the organisations that undertake a
reengineering effort do not achieve the dramatic
results they intended.'

But that's a bit long-winded for a PowerPoint slide, especially if you want to sell something. So, the 70% myth started to take hold. Soon, almost every large corporation seemed to be boasting to its shareholders that it was reengineering. And if it wasn't, its shareholders demanded to know why. IT and management consultancy spending soared. Mechanics were everywhere.

The 70% myth took hold when Professor John Kotter from the Harvard Business School published an article entitled 'Leading Change: Why Transformation Efforts Fail' in the May–June 1995 issue of the *Harvard Business Review*[13]. Oddly, this article is still frequently referenced as the origin of the 70% figure, despite not having mentioned any number. What he did write was:

> *'I have watched more than 100 companies try to remake themselves into significantly better competitors ... a few of these corporate change efforts have been very successful. A few have been utter failures. Most fall somewhere in between, with a distinct tilt toward the lower end of the scale.'*

He is, however, bolder in his follow-up book, *Leading Change*[14], published in 1995. In that book, he writes:

> *'From years of study, I estimate today more than 70% of needed change either fails to be launched, even though some people clearly see the need, fails to be completed, even though some people exhaust themselves trying, or finishes over budget, late and with initial aspirations unmet.'*

In both the article and the book, Kotter set out an eight-step recipe for success:

1. Establishing a sense of urgency.

2. Forming a powerful coalition.

3. Creating a vision.

4. Communicating the vision.

5. Empowering others to act on the vision.

6. Planning for and creating short-term wins.

7. Consolidating improvements and producing still more change.

8. Institutionalising the new approach.

Unlike reengineering, Kotter's approach prioritised the people aspects of change projects. However, as you can see from the eight steps, it is a top-down, sequential approach.

Kotter's formula quickly made its way on to management consultancy PowerPoint slides and into boardrooms. Since then, it has trickled down from the top-tier consultancies, becoming the de facto standard for enlightened change management.

Kotter updated his recipe when he returned the pages of the Harvard Business Review in November 2012, with an article entitled *Accelerate*[15]. He wrote that the eight sequential steps, set out in 1994, should be pursued in parallel.

Yet, from what I have seen, most training courses and management consultants are still promulgating the eight sequential steps. As recently as last year, I was asked to formulate 'change management' training for a niche management consultancy firm. At the top of their wish list was Kotter's eight sequential steps.

What links J.C. Penny, business process reengineering and Kotter's eight steps is that they orient leaders towards top-down, big-budget and big-bet projects, with formal leaders as heroes in a hurry.

Summary

If you want to make a successful, sustainable change:

Think and act like gardener, NOT a mechanic.

If that already makes intuitive sense to you, I hope this book will provide you with the inspiration to think about what that means for you in your context.

If you don't agree or you are not quite there yet, I hope I can provide you with the motivation to try some small-scale, small-bet experiments to find out what works for you and what doesn't. That's the essence of gardening.

In the next chapter, I am going to expand on each of three overlapping ecosystem characteristics:

- Unpredictability
- Interdependence
- Limits of control

That will complete the first part of the book, which is largely about concepts. The second part of the book contains examples, using tools and ideas, that illustrate how you can apply *The Elements of Gardening.*

Key Points

- Organisational change and personal change are two sides of the same coin.
- Organisations are like ecosystems, not machines.
- Ecosystems are characterised by unpredictability, interdependence and limits of control.
- What worked in one place might not work elsewhere … or even at the same place.
- Popular approaches to organisational change have failed to deliver expected value.
- Mechanics expect predictability; gardeners expect the unexpected.
- Mechanics tend to make big bets; gardeners make small, low-risk bets.

Ecosystem Characteristics

Unpredictability

Imagine yourself sitting in a car. You turn on the engine, put it into gear, release the brake and put your foot on the accelerator. Assuming the vehicle is well maintained, with fuel in the tank, it will accelerate in proportion to the distance you depress the pedal.

The acceleration might vary slightly, due to environmental variables such as temperature, humidity and the type of road surface. However, these variations will be within a narrow range. Your car will not go roaring off at one temperature and then crawl along at a different temperature. It has many moving parts, but it is *predictable*.

The car's moving parts are themselves made by machines. These manufacturing machines operate in tightly controlled environments. Size variation of the components, from one car to the next, is as kept as small as possible.

A machine produces the same outputs, within a narrow tolerance, from a given set of inputs. Machines are *complicated*, but they are predictable.

Contrast this with a garden. A couple of years ago, a friend gave me some beetroot seeds. I wasn't a fan of eating beetroot, so I planted them without enthusiasm, doing little to nurture or maintain the red-veined plants that sprung up.

Nonetheless, I grew a bumper crop that I felt obliged to eat. To my amazement, the freshly harvested beetroot was delicious – even raw, if cut finely enough! I became a beetroot evangelist. I bored everyone with the joys of growing and eating fresh beetroot.

The following year, I eagerly planted my beetroot seeds and carefully tended the plants that emerged. Alas, my efforts were rewarded with only a handful of misshapen beetroots.

Some months later, I was chatting to a keen vegetable gardener. I told him about my baffling beetroot failure. He sighed deeply. 'Last year was a terrible year for beetroot', he said. 'No-one had a good crop. By the way', he added after a pause, 'it's not a good idea to plant the same crop in the same beds year after year.' Doh! Crop rotation.

Unlike machines, ecosystems such as gardens are *unpredictable*. The same inputs do not always produce the same outputs. It's simply not realistic to try to control all of the environmental variables in a garden, as one can do with the components of machine.

Machines are complicated but ecosystems are complex.

In a test laboratory or on the factory floor, a car is predictable. Put a human being behind the wheel in heavy traffic and in variable weather, and the outcome is unpredictable. There are many things outside the driver's control that affect the way the car and driver perform together. This includes other drivers who have different levels of skill, tiredness and emotional stability. A car may be complicated, but traffic is complex.

It's not just factors outside your control that make things unpredictable. According to Nobel Prize-winning psychologist Daniel Kahneman[16]:

'Humans are unreliable decision makers; their judgments are strongly influenced by irrelevant factors, such as their current mood, the time since their last meal, and the weather.

Academic researchers have repeatedly confirmed that professionals often contradict their own prior judgments when given the same data on different occasions.

The unavoidable conclusion is that professionals often make decisions that deviate significantly from those of their peers, from their own prior decisions, and from rules that they themselves claim to follow.'

Kahneman cites one study, in which doctors made two assessments of the same biopsy at different times. The same doctor came to a different severity judgement 40% of the time. If that comes as a shock, here is a quote from radiology professor Leonard Berlin, writing in the medical journal *Diagnosis* in 2014[17]:

'Diagnostic errors in radiologic interpretations of plain radiographic (as well as CT, MR, ultrasound, and radionuclide) images hover in the 30% range,

31

not too dissimilar to the error rates in clinical

medicine.'

I am not suggesting that everything is unpredictable all of the time. For example, I know how long it takes me to walk to my local railway station. There is an unambiguous destination and there is a proven route that I've walked many times before. I can predict how long it will take and be correct 99% of the time. The other 1% of the time, something unforeseen might happen, such as bumping into someone who wants to chat or helping someone who has had fallen over.

After I arrive at the station, my journey to London is less predictable. The commuter rail network in the south-east of England is composed of both machines and people. Trains run late or are cancelled for a variety of reasons, from mechanical failure through to a driver not turning up. There are an enormous number of things that could go wrong. The rail network is a complex system.

The trains do, however, generally arrive and depart roughly on time (within a relatively narrow tolerance). That's because the network performs the same task, day after day, hour after hour. The individuals who work on the railway know, down to the minute, exactly what to do, how to do it, where to do it and when do it. Hopefully, they also know why!

However, in May 2018, two of the UK's regional rail companies decided to introduce a new train timetable for 46% of their train journeys. The resulting chaos lasted several weeks and was never far from the headlines. Nearly 800 train journeys were cancelled, mostly affecting people trying to get to and from work[18].

Introducing change can have unpredictable results and unforeseen consequences. Think back to China's one-child policy that I mentioned in the book's introduction. Or more prosaically, imagine that a train is cancelled, meaning that a passenger cannot get to work. Perhaps the passenger works for a business travel agency that fails to book a flight for a customer. The customer arrives at the airport to find she is not on the early-bird plane, which is now full. She misses a business meeting in Paris and her company loses the opportunity to bid for a contract that would have employed 20 people for three years. As a consequence, 10 people are made redundant, mortgage payments are due and Christmas is coming. The chain of unintended consequences could go on and on.

Change introduces unpredictability when it is introduced into complex systems, such as modern organisation and the social world in which we live.

If you want to make a change at work, the challenge is to embrace unpredictability, not try to control it.

This is what I'll talk about in the following chapters.

Interdependence

On 20 May 2020, UK Prime Minister Boris Johnson told the UK Parliament that England would have a 'world-beating track and trace system in place by 1 June, to help contain the COVID-19 pandemic'. It turned out that between May and August, the system had reached only half of the 90,000 individuals who had been in close contact with an infected person.

The creation of the system was a classic example of big-bet, big-bang machine thinking. The government had hired a specialist outsourcing company to establish the new system. In turn, the company hired 25,000 call handlers, many of them without public health experience. The call handlers were reportedly given less than a day's training before being asked to fulfil the role of contacting infected individuals in order to ask them for the contact details of those with whom they had been in close contact.

According to *The Guardian*'s Josh Halliday[19], the new system largely ignored the fact that local directors of public health already had 'small local teams of contact tracers who are absolute experts at prying really difficult and tricky information out of people' for outbreaks of diseases such as tuberculosis and sexually transmitted infections.

Public health is a devolved responsibility in the UK, so Wales, Scotland and Northern Ireland took a different approach. They looked to supplement their existing local public health tracers with community knowledge.

This contrast in approach was illustrated by an outbreak of the COVID-19 virus in a meat processing factory in Wales, where the local public health workers understood the complex web of social interdependencies. Many of the workers were immigrants whose first language was not English. Some were in the country illegally. Some wanted to speak personally to other members of their households rather than have a stranger from officialdom do it. In some households, infection was seen bringing shame on the family. And many of the workers were on zero-hours contracts, for whom self-isolation meant loss of income and an inability to feed their families. No wonder they didn't want to share information.

However, the local health workers in the small welsh town of Merthyr Tydfil worked with community leaders to understand these interdependencies and build trust, even going so far as to provide financial help for workers who would have to self-isolate.

Exercise

Let me return to the example of my failed beetroot crop to illustrate how you can think about interdependencies. Why do you think the outcomes varied between the two years? Write down the factors that you think might have prevented me from achieving the same result two years in succession.

Don't worry if you don't have any gardening knowledge; just see where your intuition takes you. Write down a couple of factors and you will find that others will follow.

How did you get on? Here's my list:

- Soil nutrients
- Air temperature
- Rainfall
- Watering
- Hours of sunlight
- Hours of direct sunlight
- Wind
- Age of seeds
- Pests
- Pest predators
- Diseases
- Insects
- Worms
- Soil aeration
- Humidity

This is not a definitive or 'correct' list; I bashed out what came into my head, just as you did. The point of the exercise isn't to come up with the right answer. Instead, it is meant to illustrate the high level of interdependence in what superficially seems like a straightforward task: plant seeds to grow delicious beetroot.

Let's say that a block of melting polar ice causes lower than usual sea temperatures in the North Atlantic. This causes storms that blow unseasonal winds towards the south coast of England in February. The clouds carried by those winds drop a record amount of rain. The rain drowns the larvae of insects that usually eat another insect that feeds on the leaves of beetroot. Bye-bye beetroot crop.

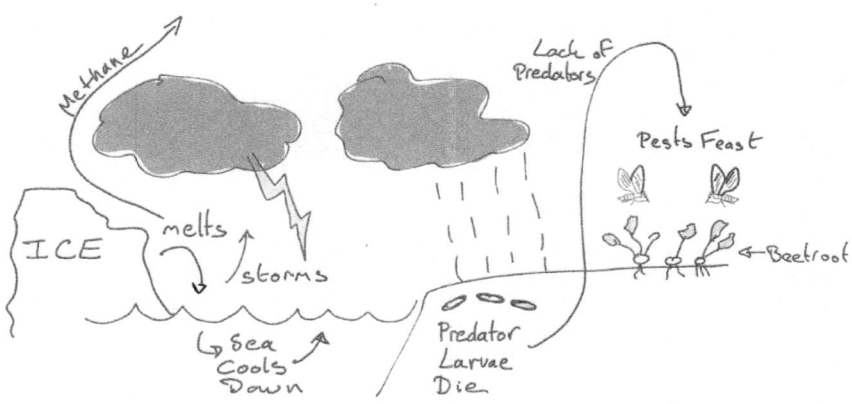

Pictures are an excellent way of thinking through interdependencies. Let me pick a different example for you to practice your skills.

Exercise

Think about an airport hotel. Make a list of factors you believe will contribute to making hotel guests happy. If you can draw them as a picture, showing the interrelationships then so much the better. After you've done that, I'll show you my attempt to do the same thing.

Now take a look at the picture below. When you start to draw relationships in this way, you will usually find that factors tumble out easily. That's because our brains store and retrieve information as a network of connections, and the picture mimics that process. Have you ever listened to a music playlist and just as a track finishes, you know what comes next? That's the brain's network of connections in action.

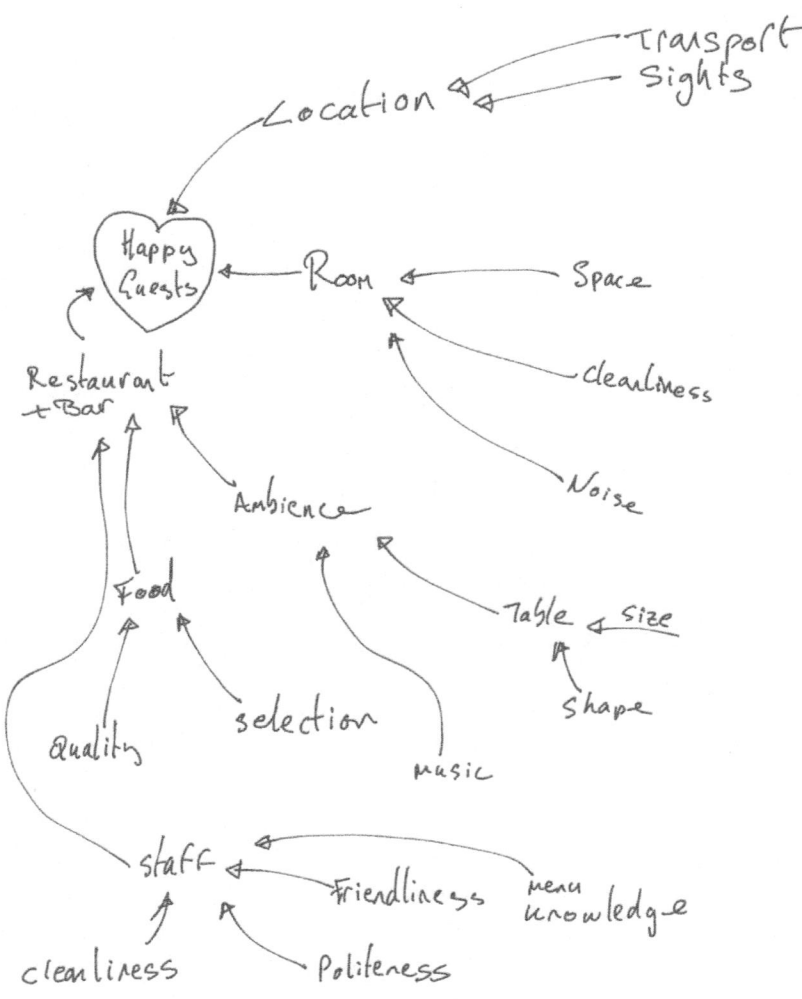

The picture above was my first pass, but it omitted something. It didn't show the financial implications of changing any of the factors show. What, for example, would be the financial implication of having larger tables and therefore possibly fewer diners at each sitting? These are what in the jargon are known as feedback loops. It's important to try to identify these because they often highlight unintended consequences. I've added in some of them in the picture below.

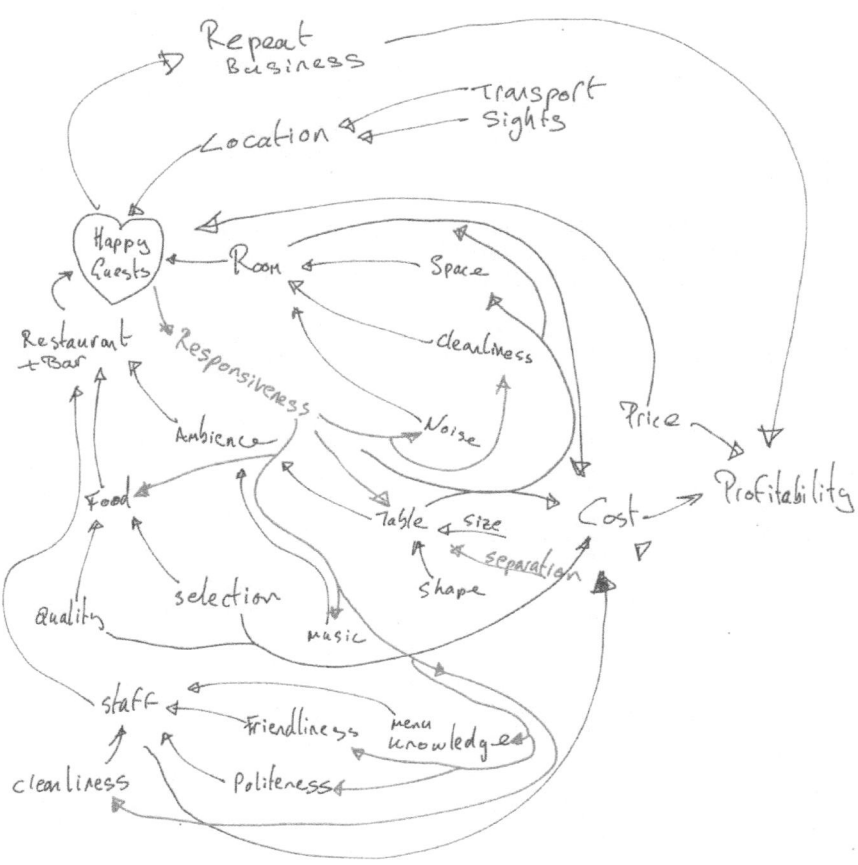

I think of these pictures as *issues-based*. They have no formal structure, and I drew each of them in less than five minutes. I just let my mind roam, looking for connections. That's something you can do on your own or in collaboration with others who will be affected by the change you are thinking of making.

I was recently coaching someone whose company wanted to promote her to a new role in a different country. One of the things I asked her to do was to draw her personal ecosystem, showing the interdependencies between the people, groups, organisations and activities in her life.

The result was a messy picture with lots of crossed lines that showed work, family, friends, recreation and voluntary work. She then labelled the arrows to show the *value* that each person receives from someone else. By value, I mean the things that are valuable to someone. Examples might include things such as:

- Love
- Friendship
- Support
- Security
- Trust
- Work
- Money
- A place to live
- Power
- Rights
- Status
- Control

Both the picture and the process of creating it helped her towards a decision. First, it brought to the surface things she might not have otherwise considered. Second, it enabled her to ask the following question: if I make a change here, could there be unintended consequences elsewhere?

Limits of Control

In his bestselling book *The 7 Habits of Highly Effective People*[20], Stephen Covey argues that there is relatively little in your work and personal life that you can control. If you try to control those things that concern you, he says, you adopt a *reactive mindset*, with a tendency to blame and complain when things don't go as you want them to.

However, he says that you can influence things that concern you. Furthermore, he argues, if you think in terms of influence rather than control, with what he calls a *proactive mindset*, you will get opportunities to expand your area of influence.

Think in terms of what you can influence, not what you can control.

I once heard the film star Tom Hanks say that his guiding principle is the advice he received right the beginning of his acting career[21]. When he joined his first theatre company, he was told 'no-one likes a squeaky wheel'. So, from that day to this, he never complained about the roles he was given or the things he was asked to do. He became known as a reliable actor with a great attitude who didn't suck in other people's emotional energy.

And because Hanks was viewed in a positive light, as someone who brought positive energy to a production and was easy to work with, he was increasingly offered better roles. Over time, he gained increasing influence over the roles he was given and the way he performed those roles. These days, of course, his presence in a film has a huge influence over the whole production. But he's still never a squeaky wheel.

This is what Covey means when he says that a proactive mindset can lead to an increased area of influence.

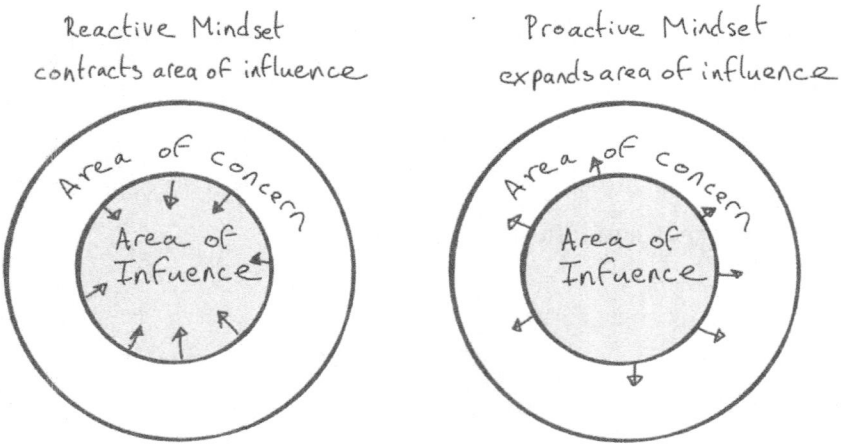

Although Covey is describing how you see the world as an individual, you can also apply his model to organisational change. Remember the hotel example in the section on interdependencies above? I took the 'concerns' from that example and mapped them on to Covey's circles, as the starting point for what is and isn't within the circle of influence.

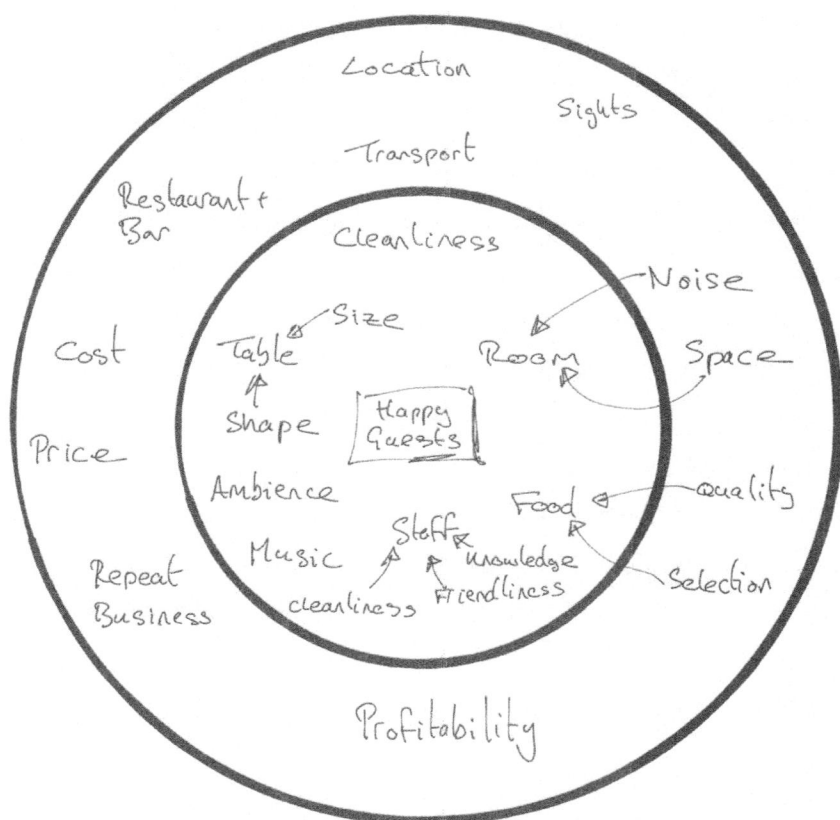

The management team might initially focus on changing things that they can influence, such as the staff, cleanliness and food. However, if they gain the confidence of the hotel's owners by improving those factors within their control, they might be given the opportunity to influence things previously outside their control, such as the menu, price per room and number of tables in the restaurant.

Beyond that, team members might have useful insights about room sizes, restaurant design and even location. If the team has been successful in improving profitability by focusing on their area of influence rather than complaining about what a terrible site they inherited, they are more likely to be heard. That, in turn, could create opportunities for the personal advancement of team members. If, for example, the owners decided to refurbish the hotel or open a new one, those high-performers, with their positive mindset, might well be first in line for plum roles.

How, practically, could the hotel team have gotten themselves to that point? They could have made 'experimental' changes, perhaps one-by-one, to those things within their area of influence, such as the food selection and its quality, music, staff training and restaurant layout. Small changes would allow them to monitor the results of those experiments and to watch out for unintended consequences. Once those things have shown demonstrable improvements, they could move on to experimenting with pricing and transport. That's a gardening approach.

In contrast, a mechanic might see a failing hotel, look at what works elsewhere and embark on a total refurbishment – in other words, to reengineer. Mechanics tend to make big bets, but gardeners make small bets.

Incidentally, I like to use the term 'experiment' rather than 'test' or 'pilot' because it's a mindset thing. A pilot is something we do to test a solution we think will work, in a limited way, before putting it into production. Experiments, however, are designed to get information. An experiment might address a piece of a puzzle, but might not necessarily try to solve the whole puzzle. Trial and error is the approach that designers take when they build prototypes of products in order to explore how to solve tricky problems.

It's a mindset that avoids thinking in terms of success or failure. It helps to avoid the common trap of confirmation bias: seeing the evidence that supports what you hope for and discounting that which doesn't.

In his excellent book *The Lean Startup*[22], Eric Ries tells a story about a product launch that failed. His company had spent many months developing state-of-the-art personal messaging software. When the launch day came, everyone in the company was excited to reap the fruits of their intellect and labour. However, according to Ries, no-one downloaded the software. No-one wanted it.

At that moment, he realised that, rather than spend months developing software, they could have created a webpage that would have allowed potential customers to express interest. This would have taken less than an hour. Now, every online product launch seems to begin with expressions of interest and relatively primitive prototypes, thanks to Ries' insight.

Ries advises you to identify the key assumptions that underlie your business plan and figure out ways (experiments) to validate them as soon and as cheaply as possible. Early and inexpensive validation of critical assumptions is one of the best pieces of project management advice I have ever heard.

How will you validate your critical assumptions as
quickly and as cheaply as possible?

Similarly, a team of MIT researchers, led by Professor Deborah Ancona, looked into the approach of two of the world's most consistently innovative companies, *PARC* and *Gore*[23].

PARC, a Xerox company, has been a technology innovator since 1970 and, amongst other things, has been responsible for laser printing, object-oriented programming, Ethernet networks and the graphical user interface and mouse that we still use for our desktop and laptop computers.

Gore has been a materials science innovator since 1958. It is most famous for *Gore-tex*, the breathable and waterproof fabric that is the basis for most quality outdoor clothing. However, its wires and cables were on the moon with Neil Armstrong in 1969, it made the fibre for spacesuits used for the first Shuttle astronauts in 1981 and it produced a seemingly endless stream of medical innovations, including the *GORE® HELEX Septal Occluder*, which is used to treat congenital heart defects.

A common factor to the two companies, writes the MIT team, is that 'they experiment, and they're resilient in the face of failure'. The team go on to say that 'lots of small bets are being made and employees are choosing which ones to back – that is, which project teams to join – the companies themselves become collective prediction markets that pool talent around good ideas and drain it from bad ones'.

These pre-eminent innovators are gardeners. They don't need to turn their organisations upside down with big bets because they are continually tending their gardens.

I have a couple of pieces of practical advice before leaving this topic. It seems natural to add interdependencies to the circle of influence picture for the hotel that I drew above. The downside is that it gets very messy and perhaps tricky to follow, as my attempt below demonstrates.

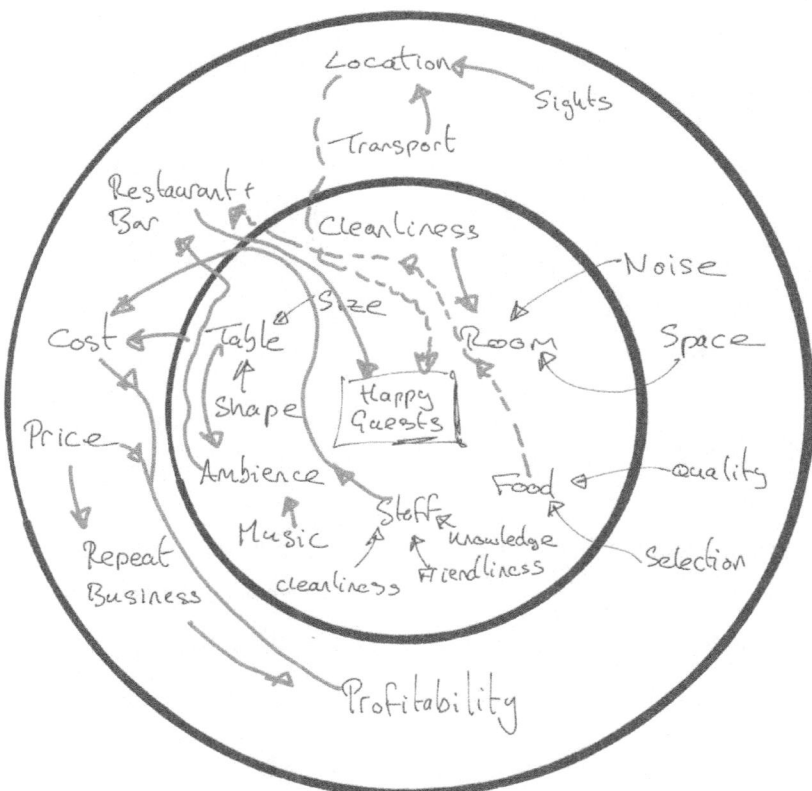

If you are comfortable with that messiness or you are doing it as a thinking process, with a team, then that's fine. The risk, however, is that you sacrifice your flow of thought in an effort to draw an elegant picture with uncrossed lines.

Similarly, you may be tempted to start with two empty circles and draw your interdependencies within those, rather than the free-flowing example I drew in the previous section. I strongly advise against drawing the circles first.

My experience is that the borders of the circles will constrain your thoughts. You will get sucked into thinking about what you can and cannot influence before you have brainstormed the factors you need to think about. You'll also be subconsciously trapped within frames that deter you from making messy-looking connections.

I would suggest drawing a free-flowing dependency picture first, before moving on to considerations of influence. If you are in a workshop setting, you can always use Post-its for items and then transfer them to the circles. However, don't forget to take a picture of the dependency picture before you do so.

The Elements of Gardening

Up until this point, I have illustrated the core ideas in this book using other people's experiences of change. However, before you delve into the second part of the book, I'd like you to think about how you can apply those ideas to a real change that you would like to make. Henceforth, I'll simply refer to it as *your change*.

Your change could be absolutely anything. It could be a change you want to make at work, or it could be a personal or professional change. It could be a significant change or small incremental change. If you approach the material in this book with an open and creative mind, I guarantee you will find your thoughts going down paths that would otherwise have remained unexplored. The only criterion for choosing your project is that it is something real and important to you.

If you start to think about your change now, you will get a double benefit. First, when you apply the ideas in this book to something meaningful to you, it will bring those ideas more vividly to life than any example that I can give you. Second, by the end of the book, you will have done the work to think deeply about your change and will perhaps even start to make it happen. So, let's begin that process now.

Exercise

Think about your change and ask yourself these three questions:

1. What are the interdependencies?
2. What is and isn't within your control?
3. What is and isn't predictable?

Try drawing a picture similar to the hotel example give earlier.

In the rest of the book, I aim to help you answer three questions:

- How can you create an adaptable plan that responds to the unforeseen?
- How can you conduct experiments, build prototypes and run pilots to explore uncertainty?
- How can you be alert for unintended and unexpected consequences?

As I said in the introduction, those examples will be based around a framework, named 'The Elements of Gardening'. Here's a reminder of that framework:

- Plan
- Prepare the soil

- Plant
- Prune
- Weed
- Water
- Stake
- Ensure good health
- Enjoy the harvest

Scientists and innovators often use analogies to explore and discover new ideas by using concepts that are already familiar – for example, asking yourself 'what would "prepare the soil" mean in this context of your change?' Once you find the first answer, you'll find your mind going down paths you would not otherwise have explored. This is a particularly powerful way of thinking when you do it in collaboration with others.

No analogy is perfect, but you can push it until it breaks and you will get a lot of new insights along the way.

I'll explore each element of gardening in turn, but this does not imply they take place sequentially. If you want to make sustainable change, all of the elements need your attention, all of the time, as they do at PARC and Gore.

Before moving on to the second part of the book, there are a couple of essential points that I would like to make. First, thinking like a gardener doesn't mean you have to throw away a mechanic's toolset. Objective data, design and engineering are the bedrock of experimentation.

Second, approaching change as a gardener does not mean you have to eschew radical change. As the old saying goes, you eat an elephant one bite at a time. Let's have a look at a couple of short examples that show how a gardening approach achieved radical changes, with a robust scientific basis.

In 1991, three researchers from MIT published a book entitled *The Machine That Changed the World[24]*. It was the culmination of a five-year study that sought to understand how Japanese automotive manufacturers, and *Toyota* in particular, had achieved global leadership. The book introduced the term *Lean Production* and led to a worldwide revolution in manufacturing across all industries.

At the core of Lean Production is what the Japanese call *Kaizen*, meaning continuous improvement. You probably already know the Kaizen improvement cycle: *Plan-Do-Check-Act*. You run small experiments to find out what makes an improvement to a process and what doesn't.

The foundation of Kaizen at Toyota is the data visualisation approach known as *Statistical Process Control*, which was introduced to Japan by two US engineers, W. Edwards Demming[25] and Joseph Juran[26]. It ensures that factory-floor workers can differentiate between systematic and one-off problems, so that effort is focused on making fundamental changes rather than chasing ghosts. For Toyota, all of these incremental improvements added up to a *machine that changed the world*. That's pretty radical.

Occasionally, however, you face one big, well-defined challenge with what appears to be a fixed completion date. Take, for example, the referendum to decide whether the UK should stay in the European Union (EU). As something scheduled to occur on one specific day in 2016, isn't a big-bet approach unavoidable? That seems to have been the conclusion of the government and the leading political parties. During the campaign that preceded the vote, they marshalled their considerable resources, and their control of the national news agenda, to paint a dire picture of the consequences of leaving. Rational arguments, they presumed, would lead to a predictably rational outcome.

The campaign to leave the EU took a different approach. Hamstrung by limited resources and less influence over the mainstream news agenda, the campaign had to innovate. Dominic Cummings, who ran the campaign to leave, explained that they crafted a series of core, emotion-based messages using all the data they could gather, including polls, doorstep conversations and focus groups[27]:

> *'We had data science people sitting at the heart of the operation and essentially taking our core messages and just running experimentally a whole bunch of different things on Facebook and elsewhere, and figuring out what things work and what things don't work. We started with relatively small amounts of money just to run this experimental process [using] exactly the same categories of demographics that Facebook used for its digital advertising platform.'*

Then, in the last two weeks of the campaign, explained Cummings, they spent nearly all of their funds on different Facebook ads, each targeting a specific undecided demographic, for whom they knew those ads resonated. Alongside this, they ran a data-driven ground campaign to ensure they got their vote out to the polling booths.

A similar approach was used by Donald Trump's campaign in the 2016 presidential election. And when Boris Johnson was elected as UK Prime Minister in 2020, Cummings was his closest advisor. Following Johnson's election success, Cummings was installed at the heart of government as Johnson's thinker-in-chief and de facto chief of staff.

Cummings's was a divisive figure in the UK. On the right of politics, he was lauded as strategic genius. On the left he is regarded as evil and rude, with little practical experience. But whether or not you agree with his politics, he was either lucky with his stewardship of the referendum and the general election, or he had perhaps understood better than others how things work.

Before he entered government, he used to write an almost impenetrable 'blog. Entries are long, frustrated streams of consciousness about public policy. Inability to express one's ideas clearly is never a good sign, but I was curious, so I persisted in reading them.

As I dug deeper, I was surprised to find myself in agreement with many of his core ideas. He believes that public policy sits within a complex system, with inherent unpredictability. He has a keen interest in using data models in order to adapt quickly to uncertainty and make informed decisions.

It's puzzling, therefore, that the UK government's response to the first nine months of the pandemic was so haphazard and continues to be so, as I write in November 2020.

Perhaps the answer lies in the warning that Mervyn King, former Governor of the Bank of England, gave us, to beware of 'bogus quantification'. Data modelling is useful as long as you don't become too attached to the models. A model is only as good as its underlying assumptions. That's why it's so important test assumptions and to revisit them regularly.

Or maybe hubris has clouded Cummings's judgement, just as it did for Ron Johnson at J. C. Penney? Dogged by a poor record of testing thus far, a leaked document shows that the government is considering a £100 billion project, to attempt to increase Covid-19 testing capacity to 10 million tests per day, by early in 2021, using technology that does not yet exist.

The project is named *Project Moonshot*[28] and, according to the document, it would "take a Manhattan Project-type approach". The type of language in the document is straight out of Cummings's 'blog. Has his gardening approach given away to the siren call of the mechanic's big-bet death grip?

In a further echo of Ron Johnson, Cumming's lasted just 10 months as Boris Johnson's chief advisor.

Key Points

- People are unpredictable and inconsistent.
- What worked before might work not the next time around.
- Seek to understand interdependencies and feedback loops (draw them).
- What is inside your area of influence?
- Don't be a squeaky wheel – increase your area of influence.
- A gardening approach can deliver radical change.

- Choose 'your change' to which you can apply the ideas in this book

Part II

The Elements of Gardening

Plan

What is Planning?

Introduction

There are three main stages of planning:

- Be clear about what you want to achieve.
- Work out how you will achieve it.
- Weigh costs versus benefits, and plan for what could go wrong (risks).

Whether it's personal or organisational change, the first of these is often poorly done. Albert Einstein is reputed to have said: 'If I had an hour to solve a problem, I'd spend 55 minutes thinking about the problem and five minutes thinking about solutions.'

It's an apocryphal quote, but it chimes with the experience of seasoned executives. In a recent survey, 85% of C-suite executives said that problem diagnosis is a significant issue for their organisation. The researcher Thomas Wedell-Wedellsborg, writing the January–February 2017 issue of the *Harvard Business Review*, writes[29]:

*'Spurred by a penchant for action, managers tend to
switch quickly into solution mode without checking
whether they really understand the problem.'*

In my experience, 'solution mode' doesn't usually equate to a process of generating and evaluating a wide range of different solutions. It usually means 'decide quickly on a solution, so we can start doing things, rather than sitting around talking about doing things'. Ask to see the *plan* and it's most likely you will be shown a *schedule* of who will do what, why, when, where and how.

It's not just organisational change that suffers from the tendency 'to switch quickly into solution mode'. Ask someone about their career plan and they will usually describe a vague goal, before jumping forward to describe the steps needed to get there. In my experience, people at a career crossroads often describe what they don't want, based on their current role, rather than what they do want. Rarely do I come across someone who has thought deeply about what would make them happy at work and in life.

What can gardeners teach us about planning? If you ask to see a gardener's plan for a new garden, they are likely to describe what they want from their garden and perhaps a proposed layout. If they represent a schedule for the work, it will probably be a high-level one that's easily adapted to the weather. By schedule I mean who is going to do what, where and when.

For example, a gardener might say that they want their garden to supply a year-round supply of vegetables, but also to have lots of flowers and be welcoming to wildlife and insects. That's what I would call the *purpose*.

The gardener might amplify that by saying there will be a vegetable garden at the far end of the garden and then, along the south-facing wall before that, there will be a herbaceous border with only white flowers. The north-facing wall will be populated by shade-tolerant shrubs, and adjacent to the back of the house will be a patio, herb garden and a pond with Koi Carp. That's what I would call the *vision*.

The gardener's vision brings the desired outcome to life. It's something we can see in our mind's eye, in living, moving colour.

If the gardener is a professional gardener, they might show their client drawings and sample photographs in order to achieve a shared understanding of the outcome. This *shared vision* conjures up a mental picture of what it is like to step into that garden: what it looks like, how it smells and how it sounds. If there is more than one person working in that garden, the purpose and the shared vision will guide the choices they make as they create the garden.

Note that the vision is broad enough to allow for a range of different designs, but it already contains some design decisions, or *constraints*, such as where the vegetable garden will be located. That is something I'll address in the next section when I describe how purpose and vision worked together to create the iPhone.

The Origin of the iPhone

Bob Borchers, a member of the team that created the iPhone, told Californian students[30]:

> *'The challenge Steve [Jobs] laid out for us when we created the iPhone wasn't to make a touch-screen device that would play apps and do all of this stuff.*
>
> *His [charge] was simple. He wanted to create the first phone that people would fall in love with.*
>
> *Now if you're an engineer, like I am by training, you're like, what the heck does that mean?*
>
> *But he was right. The idea was he wanted to create something that was so instrumental and integrated in people's lives that you'd rather leave your wallet at home than your iPhone. The product had to be a revolutionary mobile phone that let users carry 'the internet in their pocket', the latter of which was somewhat of a foreign concept at the time.'*

Downloadable apps, photographs, video and GPS were not part of the *vision*; they were solutions that the team created to fulfil the *vision*. Steve Jobs gave his team a *purpose* and *vision* that allowed plenty of scope for innovation.

The Purpose:

To create the first phone that people would fall in love with.

The Vision:

Something that was so instrumental and integrated in people's lives that you'd rather leave your wallet at home than your iPhone. A revolutionary mobile phone that let users carry the internet in their pocket.

There are important lessons here for budding gardeners:

- Both statements describe customer value, not a list of features and functions.
- Both statements invoke emotion.
- The *vision* conjures up a mental picture of the customer value.
- The fewer the constraints, the more numerous the potential solutions.

Consider the purpose. When the iPhone launched in 2007, the notion of anyone *loving* a phone was preposterous. Mobile phones were cheap commodity items. Before the iPhone, no-one queued around the block for phones. Steve Balmer, then CEO of Microsoft, is captured in a YouTube video laughing at the 'ridiculous notion that anyone would pay $500 for a phone'[31].

Now think about the iPhone vision described above. Have you ever lost your phone? How did you *feel*? The thread of emotion, from the purpose and through the vision, isn't there by chance. There is a 91-second Apple marketing video[32], which begins:

'*The first question we ask is what do we want people to feel?*'

Those 91 seconds fundamentally changed the way I think about change at work. Start with emotion.

Google and Microsoft seem to begin their design process, as mechanics usually do, by asking: 'what functions and features do people want?' If you've ever used Microsoft Word, you'll know where that leads you.

Some of us are old enough to remember when MP3 players first came on to the market, with their mass of function buttons and small menu-intensive screens. They were geeky, niche products until the iPod came along in 2001 and made it simple to download and play MP3s. Steve Jobs described that first iPod as something that lets you carry '1,000 songs in your pocket'.

The very best visions create a mental picture, with some combination of sound, touch, smell and taste. It's like a movie trailer in your head. Sometimes this takes quite a lot of description, as you'll see when I talk about the Sony Walkman in the chapter 'Stake'.

However, the iPhone *vision* has relatively few words because it uses concepts that we already understand – concepts such as a phone, the internet, a pocket and the notion of being on the move. Think about what it would have been like to read the iPhone vision before smartphones existed? You imagine yourself walking; you take your phone from your pocket to find information, to communicate or to entertain.

It's also worth noting that the iPhone vision is abstract enough to give the designers creative freedom. However, also worth noting is that the vision does contain a couple of subtle *constraints.* First, it's a phone. That may seem obvious now, but think about Google Glasses or the Apple Watch. Had Steve Jobs asked for a communication device and not specified a phone, the team may have ended up somewhere else.

The second constraint was that the phone had to be small enough to fit in a typical pocket. Also, seemingly obvious now, but without that constraint, the designers might have ended up somewhere else, say an iPad. It also implies something about the weight of the device.

The two constraints together seem, with the benefit of hindsight, to make the iPhone design inevitable. Yet that wasn't the case in 2007, when the BlackBerry and its tiny physical keyboard seemed invincible. But as Sir Jonathan Ive, Apple's former head of design, said: 'after you have seen a great design, you can't imagine it being any other way'.

That question – *what do we want people to feel?* – is so powerful that it's worth pausing for a moment to consider how it might apply to your change. Whether your change is a big organisational one or something more personal, the question will challenge you to think deeply about your change.

If it's a personal change, you might ask yourself: 'what do I want people to say about me when I leave the room?'

- Likeable?
- Trustworthy?
- Reliable?
- Detailed?
- Team player?
- Control freak?

If it's an organisational change, think about how you want those affected to feel once the change has happed. We'll cover this in a lot more detail in the chapter 'Prepare the Soil'.

In the next two sections, I am going to dig a bit deeper into purpose and vision because they are so foundational for successful change.

After that, I'll share some thoughts about scheduling, costs versus benefits and thinking about what could go wrong.

Shared Purpose

There are three main ways you can define 'purpose'.

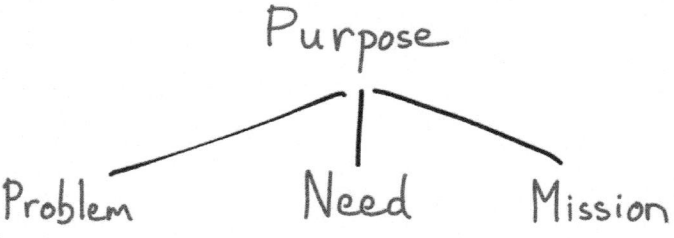

Sometimes, each is a slightly different way of stating the same thing:

- Problem: lack of clean drinking water is a significant cause of death in developing nations.
- Need: clean drinking water for families living on less than $1–2 per day.
- Mission: reduce by half the proportion of people without sustainable access to safe drinking water.

Some people like to always define purpose as a problem. They will reframe a mission or need as 'a problem statement'. This has some merit, as it's an effective way to transform a vague purpose into a crisp, measurable outcome that begs the question: 'how will you know if you have solved the problem?'

However, if you always define purpose as a problem, you can get trapped by language that describes what you don't want rather than what you do want. And that can narrow your options.

Think back to the iPhone example. If you had asked BlackBerry users about their biggest problem, it would probably have been the size of the keyboard. It's pretty unlikely they would have complained that they couldn't surf the internet or use GPS to navigate their journeys.

Remember the iPhone's purpose statement? *To create the first phone that people would fall in love with.* That's a *mission* that offers a wide range of solutions. It's tricky to reframe it as a problem.

Marketing has taught us to think in terms of *unmet needs* in order to open up thinking. Think in terms of selling holes, not drills, said Philip Kotler way back in 1967. Focus on the need, not the product[33].

Each of the three ways of defining purpose (problem, need or mission) is equally valid, but I suggest you try to word your *purpose* as all three in order to see if you discover anything new in a different frame. Then choose the one that resonates best for your change.

I also suggest you test your definition of purpose, using what is known as *the five whys*. The idea is that you ask the question 'why?' up to five times to get to the root of something. It originated as a problem-solving technique in the *Toyota Production System*, but it's equally applicable to a mission or a need as it is for a problem.

For example, as I write, the UK government has just decided to invest £100 billion in high-speed rail links in order to shorten train journey times between a handful of major cities[34]. It's a controversial decision because of escalating costs, doubts about the benefits and a question over consistency with the government carbon emission targets.

The original project budget in 2012 was £33 billion. To date, the project has already spent £7 billion. Also, the project will not improve daily workers' commute into the cities from surrounding towns and suburbs. The project is about inter-city, not intra-city travel.

If you examine the project's purpose using the five whys, *the first why* might be: why do you want to spend £100 billion to link major cities by rail?

The answer, from the 2012 business case, is 'to shorten train journey times between major cities and to increase capacity for those journeys'.

The second why might be: why you want to shorten train journey times and increase capacity?

The answer, also based on the 2012 business case, is that shorter journey times will make business travellers more productive and generate a benefit of £2.40 for every pound spent (the 2020 review says that benefit figure looks likely to drop to £1.50 for every pound).

For *the third why*, you might ask: why does a faster journey time between major cities make business travellers more productive?

I don't know the answer to that, but something I read suggested that the authors of the business case assumed that the time spent on the train was unproductive. Or perhaps it was an assumption that people needed to get to meetings more easily (remember this isn't about the daily commute)?

The fourth why might be: why do you think that time on the train is unproductive? Or if it was about meetings, you might ask: why do people have to travel to meetings? This is a question that has become more obvious to ask since the COVID-19 pandemic.

I will not labour the point by inventing a fifth why, as I am sure you can see how the five whys work. As you go up the hierarchy of whys, each step prompts you to examine assumptions and consider alternative solutions.

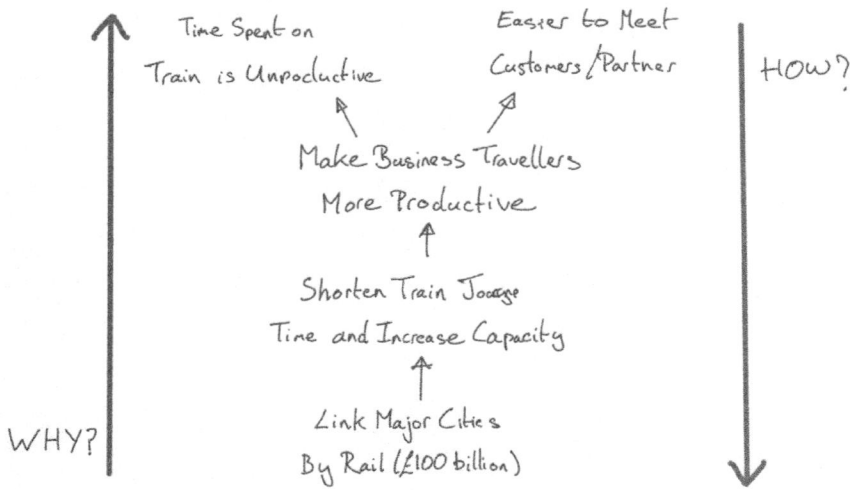

I'm not going to rehearse the argument for and against, as I just want to illustrate the value you get when you take time to define and scrutinise purpose. This example also illustrates the value of regularly revisiting assumptions. The project was approved by the UK Parliament on 23 February 2020. On 6 March 2020, the UK experienced its first death from COVID-19. I wonder how often the business case assumptions will be revisited in order to ensure they are still valid?

The Five Whys can help you to check whether you are heading in the right direction at any stage of a project.

On one occasion, in my role as an independent consultant, I was asked to review a sizeable IT-based project that was in trouble. When I met the

Project Sponsor, he told me that the project had an 'absolutely fixed' deadline. The Project Sponsor told me he had lost confidence in the Project Manager, who had said publicly that the deadline was unachievable.

The sponsor wanted me to spend a week reviewing the project and make recommendations to 'get it back on track', including personnel changes where necessary. I had many questions for the sponsor, but he didn't have time to answer them and suggested I talk to his PA get whatever I needed.

The PA connected me to the Project Manager, who I met over coffee. Rather than ask why she thought the project would miss the deadline, I wanted to know why the organisation was doing the project. *This was the first of my five whys.*

She told me that the goal of the project was to replace an existing system that analysed information feeds from a variety of financial exchanges.

This prompted *my second why*: why did the old system need replacing? The Project Manager didn't know, but suggested that the sponsor's PA had her finger on the pulse of everything in which the sponsor was involved.

I returned to talk to the PA, whose PA role was just one stop on her fast-track development path around the organisation. She explained that the project came about when the supplier of the product at the core of the existing system announced a 50% increase in the annual licence fee.

I asked *my third why*: why was the increase an issue for the organisation? The PA raised her eyebrows and fell silent. I broke a long pause by asking whether the new project would result in a significant cost saving.

She confided that the financial case was marginal. So, I asked *my fourth why*: why was the organisation pursuing a project that could cost it money? She said she didn't know, but was being discreet and suggested I talk to the supplier.

The supplier's Account Manager told me that they had increased the price because all of their other customers had migrated over to a newer and better product. However, my client, the sponsor, had refused to change and was now the only customer using the old product. Rather than terminate support, the Account Manager told me, he had offered to support the old product at cost because his company valued the relationship.

I asked why for the fifth occasion: why did the sponsor decide to pursue an internal solution? The supplier didn't know, except that the sponsor 'went ballistic' and said he would refuse to pay the increase, in the full knowledge that there wasn't an alternative supplier.

When I caught up with the sponsor a few days after our initial conversation, I asked why the project had a fixed deadline. His body language told me he didn't welcome the question. So I asked whether the licence renewal date was driving the project deadline. He told me brusquely that it wasn't relevant to what he had asked me to do.

I knew what I was about to say next would not go down well. I recommended he cancel the project, pay the increased licence fee to buy time, and evaluate the cost and timescale to migrate to the supplier's new product.

His response was colourful and I made a fast exit. I thought my advice would save much money, but my invoice went unpaid. I decided not to pursue it.

I kept my ear to the ground and some months later I heard that the project had missed its deadline. The organisation had paid the increased licence fee and three months later had cancelled the project. The sponsor, previously regarded as a rising star, left the company shortly afterwards. To most people's surprise, his PA took over his role, being promoted ahead of more experienced executives.

As this example illustrates, asking why five times doesn't necessarily mean you ask all of the questions of just one person. Nor should you expect to get the same answer from each person you ask. There are also different whys that I could have asked that would have led down different paths. The five whys approach isn't a magic potion that presents the solution on a plate; you still have to use your judgement to reconcile different views.

It's also important to remember that the answers you get may be emotional rather than rational, even when dressed up as logical. If I had the opportunity to ask the sponsor why five times, he was unlikely to have volunteered that he initiated the project simply because the price hike bruised his ego.

As Rory Sutherland, co-founder of Ogilvy's behavioural science practice, points out in his entertaining book *Alchemy: The Surprising Power of Ideas That Don't Make Sense*, motivations are often unconscious[35].

Our conscious minds are skilled at coming up with rationalisations after the event. You have to gather multiple perspectives and be aware, like a doctor, that the presented problem might not be the real cause of distress.

In Sutherland's book, he tells a story about an energy provider that services and repairs home heating boilers. Unfortunately, the time needed to repair a boiler is unpredictable. Thus, the company gives the customer a half-day appointment window, which is either before or after midday.

We've all experienced this and it's annoying. You sit indoors all day wondering when, or if, the engineer will turn up. Ask customers how to improve the service and they'll say they want a narrower time window.

The Ogilvy team hypothesised that the issue wasn't the size of the time window as such, but rather the feeling of uncertainty: not being able to sit in the garden or go to the shop, just in case the engineer pushes the doorbell at that precise moment.

Ogilvy proposed to its client that the engineers send customers a text half an hour before arrival. Sutherland says the company told the client: 'this was one of the solutions we propose to test'.

I like this story for a few reasons:

- Unconscious motivations are rarely volunteered in response to the question 'why?'.
- The team were not fixated on a single 'best' option.
- If you want to test an unconscious motivation hypothesis, you will have to run some experiments.

Exercise

Try the following exercise for your change:

Describe the purpose of your change in the three different ways, as a:

- Problem
- Need
- Mission

Ask yourself the five whys for each of these.

Shared Vision

Purpose is the most abstract description of the change you want to make. To get to a solution, you need to start asking how you might fulfil the purpose. A vision is the next step on that journey towards a solution. It brings to life what the world will look like after the change. It describes the benefits of the change, not the technical nuts and bolts that deliver those benefits.

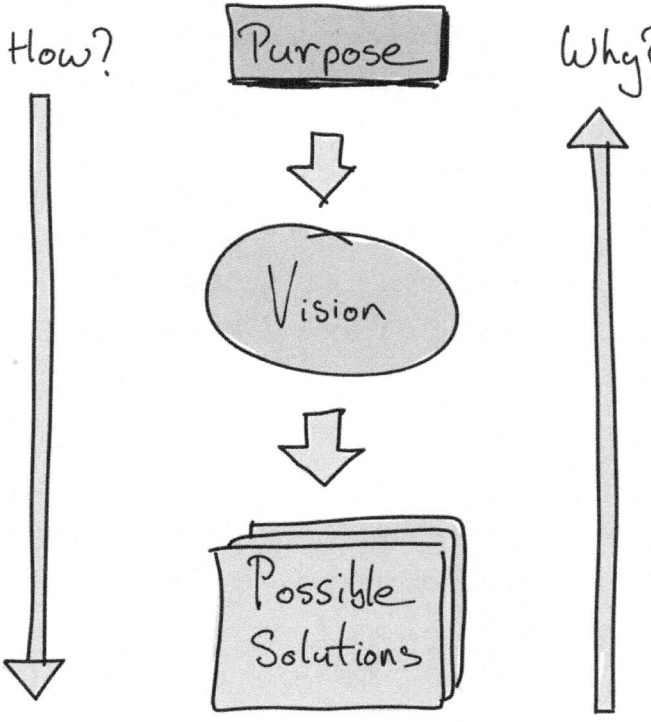

It's often difficult to describe the vision without including some element of a solution. However, the fewer elements of a solution in your vision, the greater the number of possible solutions that can flow from it. I call those elements of a solution *constraints* because they constrain the range of solutions available.

Remember the iPhone. The two constraints were that it had to be a phone that fitted in a regular pocket. However, there was nothing else to constrain design choices. The vision was to carry the internet in your pocket. Apps and GPS were solutions to fulfil the vision.

If you decide to introduce constraint*s* into your vision, do so explicitly. Write down the constraint and why you decided to introduce it. All too often, implicit constraints are introduced and baked in as a result of untested assumptions. If, however, you make them explicit, it allows someone to revisit and challenge those constraints, perhaps by asking the five whys!

When I am working with clients, I ask them to draw a picture of their vision, not just to paint a picture using words. A picture, especially in colour, engages many more areas of the brain than language can do alone. A picture is also ideal for collaborative working on a flip chart or whiteboard.

My favourite way to describe a vision is the 'movie poster'. Below is an example I did with my sister-in-law, Ulrike, for her excellent book on collaboration, *So geht WIRTSCHAFT!* It is intended to show a vision for local village shops collaborating to compete with online food retailers. You can see that, the bicycle aside, I have tried to keep constraints, or elements of solutions, out of the picture.

Green Delivery

Starring Your Local Shops

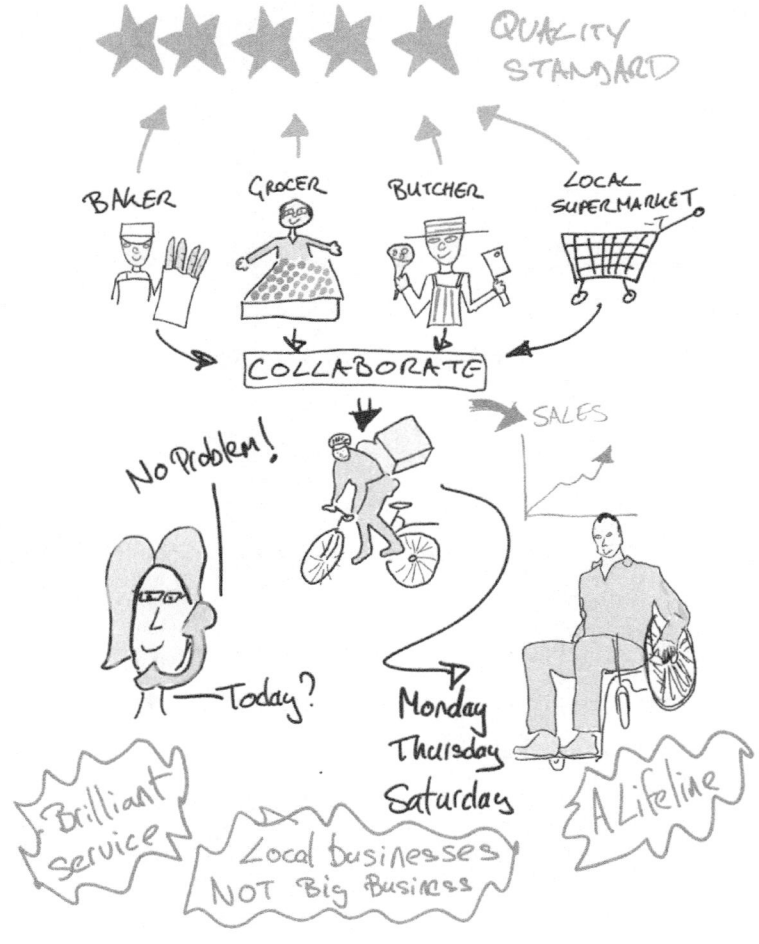

When I am coaching a client at a career crossroads, I'll ask them to close their eyes and imagine themselves in the future, in three or five years. I'll ask them to tell me what they can see and hear, and how they feel.

Someone I know was a London policeman who had a dilemma. The Australian police force was on a recruiting drive. My friend had been approached to move Down Under, with his family, all relocation expenses paid. It was an enticing offer: sun, sea and a less challenging 'clientele'. However, all of his friends and family were in London, so it was a big decision.

I suggested he and his family create a movie poster. Being a rational type of person, he laughed and dismissed the idea as woo-woo. However, one wet Sunday afternoon, after a week of misunderstandings and family rows, he found himself drawing two competing visions on the back of a roll of wallpaper in order to try to explain what was in his head.

After he finished, his wife picked up the Sharpie and started to add to the competing visions. She also made a few changes, but not before asking her husband and the children in order to get their agreement. It wasn't long before their two young children were drawing on the pictures.

The family kept the two pictures on the kitchen wall for a week, discussing, embellishing and changing the competing visions. By the end of the week, they had described what they wanted from a new life in Australia – a shared vision of benefits they wanted from the change. It turned out that their children's views had the greatest influence on what they wanted as a family.

My friend, the policeman, talked to the Australian police force and described what his family needed in order to be able to agree to make a move. He wasn't brave enough to show them the actual drawing, by the way. There was a bit of negotiation, but terms were agreed, including a business-class trip for the paternal grandparents during the first year.

I am pleased to report that, 10 years later, the family are happy and well. Their grandparents often visit to see their son and their Aussie grandchildren. Each time they visit, they seem to stay a little longer.

In his seminal book *The Fifth Discipline*[36], MIT academic Peter Senge introduced the idea of *The Learning Organisation*. In that book, he writes about the importance of a shared vision:

> *'A vision is truly shared when you and I have a*
> *similar picture and are committed to one another*
> *having it, not just each of us, individually, having it.*
> *When people truly share a vision they are connected,*
> *bound together by a common aspiration.'*

A shared vision acts as the true north for your project team. It:

- Describes the outcome you are seeking to achieve.
- Engages stakeholders in its creation and delivery.
- Serves as a basis for generating alternative solutions.
- Guides decisions and actions.

Below are some tools you can use to create a shared vision.

The Movie Poster

What is the primary image on the poster? What is the one-sentence headline? Who are the main characters? What are the quotes from the critics? What emotions do you aim to evoke? Does sit have a theme song?

The Cover Story

The cover story is a similar idea to the movie poster, except that the output is the cover of a popular tabloid newspaper, with punchy headlines, subheadings and quotes. As before, think about the characters and the sort and the emotions aroused.

Design the Box

In this variation, you define the packaging for a box that describes a new service, for example, with appropriate graphics, a description of the benefits and quotes from happy customers. Think about the adverts for seemingly amazing products in your social media feeds. Benefits, benefits, benefits.

TV Advert or Movie Trailer

I have used these tools to good effect in tandem with the movie poster. A team starts by drawing the movie poster on a flip chart and then moves on to storyboard the movie trailer, including the suggested soundtrack. The soundtrack choices are often very revealing.

Exercise

Practise your visioning skills by thinking about your future. Imagine yourself outside your home in three years' time:

- Describe your home and the immediate vicinity.
- What do you see, hear, smell, and feel?
- Imagine opening the front door and walking inside.
- How does that feel?

Imagine entering each room in turn. What do you see, hear, smell and feel?

Or better still, draw a movie poster. Perhaps share it with those close to you. Ask them to help shape your vision and their role in it.

Schedule

When you have determined your purpose and vision, the next step is to define a schedule of work to realise them.

The main lesson from gardening is to create a flexible schedule that you can adapt to changing circumstances. You may decide when you would like to plant your tomato seedlings outside, but exactly when you do so will depend on the weather. Or if a disease blights a particular plant, you may want to substitute it with a different species.

This is probably how you already approach relatively small and personal changes. However, when you need to collaborate with other people in order to achieve your vision and purpose, you need to create a shared understanding of who is going to do what, where and when. And that means writing it down in some form or other. The traditional way of doing this is with a *Gantt* (or bar) chart or sometimes a *PERT* chart. These are often used in tandem, with a Gantt chart best at showing the timeline and a PERT chart best at showing dependencies, with earliest and latest start and finish dates.

Gantt Chart

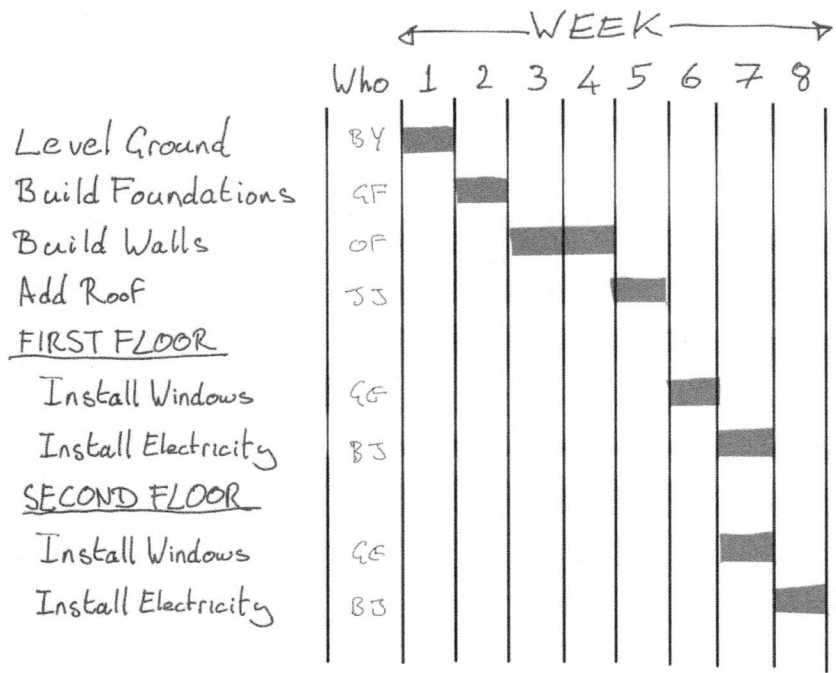

PERT Chart

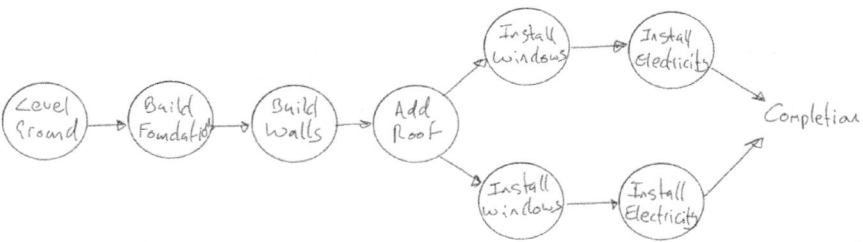

I believe that these are useful tools if kept at a relatively high level. However, as the size and complexity of a change increases, there is a tendency to create commensurately complex charts that contain a spurious degree of accuracy. Often these charts take so much time to develop and maintain that there is a reluctance to adapt them to changing circumstances. The leaders of such projects end up trying to bend the world to their schedule rather than bend the schedule to fit the world.

This is summarised beautifully at *West Point*, the elite military academy in the US, where students are taught that:

'No battle plan survives contact with the enemy.'

This quote paraphrases something written in 1871 by Field Marshall Helmuth Carl Bernard Graf von Moltke[37], the man who created the template for modern warfare. West Point's Tom Kolditz explains[38]:

'Over time we've come to understand more and more what makes people

successful in complex operations. You may start off trying to fight your

plan but the enemy gets a vote. Unpredictable things happen.'

To counter this unpredictability, West Point tells students that they must write *the Commander's Intent* at the very top of every battle plan. The Commander's Intent describes what Kolditz calls *the end state* – or, put another way, the purpose and *vision.* So, when the unexpected happens on the battlefield, as it inevitably does, decisions and actions are guided by the Commander's Intent, not a detailed, blow-by-blow list of instructions whose validity is long past.

So, what's the alternative? I'm aware of three approaches. The first two originated in software development, with so-called *agile* practices. The third comes from the construction industry's desire to learn from *lean manufacturing*:

- Kanban
- Scrum
- The Last Planner System

I've included a brief overview of each in Appendix B, 'Schedule Approaches'. The three approaches share one common factor, which is *visualising the work*. The schedule is posted up on the wall where everyone can see and discuss it. Work items are usually written on Post-it notes that can easily be changed and rearranged. When something gets stuck, team members gather around and figure out how to unblock it.

And although I have been writing about schedules in the context of large projects, many people (myself included) use this sort of approach to manage their personal workload. I like the ability to see all of the things I want to do in one visual space and to be able to rearrange them, depending on priority and energy level.

Costs, Benefits and Risks

If you agree with me that change is inherently unpredictable, then it follows that both the cost of and benefit from a change are also inherently unpredictable.

This unpredictability creates a problem for significant organisational changes that usually demand a business case. And the more significant the change, the less accurate a forecast is likely to be. And, let's face it, proponents of large-scale change are usually over-optimistic. When did you last hear of a major project coming in under budget?

The solution is to change the way you arrive at cost and timescale estimates. Instead of asking 'what's the cost of this list of stuff I want in my vision?', ask:

'What can I get for the money I have to spend that's consistent with the vision?'

Then break the work down into usable chunks of benefit, each chunk with a best guess of the time and cost needed to deliver it. If it were a garden, each chunk would deliver something useful, such as a fish pond, a flower bed or vegetable bed. And then, as each piece is delivered, you can compare the estimated cost and time with the actual values. If there is a difference, you can investigate why and, if necessary, extrapolate the estimating error to the remainder of the work. You also get a chance to evaluate how well you work with your collaborators and make changes if you don't work well together.

If after a couple of chunks of value are delivered, you find it is going to cost a lot more than you expected, at least you found out sooner rather than later. You now have a choice. You can increase your budget to cover everything initially scheduled or you can decide to do less work and stay within budget. If you choose the latter, at least you will have some practical value rather than waiting until the very end.

An approach that delivers regular chunks of value is the best way I know of mitigating the risk of cost and schedule overrun. It's the same gardening principle that runs through this book. Keep risk low by running small-scale experiments to test key assumptions.

There are, of course, many other types of risk, such as whether enough customers will buy the product or whether the change of process will reduce the cost as expected. The other side of risk is usually an untested assumption. Your challenge is to find ways of testing the most critical assumptions as quickly and cheaply as possible. And don't forget to keep checking them, as the world around you is forever changing.

Exercise

Write down the three key assumptions upon which your change depends. How will you test them as quickly and as cheaply as possible?

Key Points

- A clear shared purpose and vision is the essence of a good plan.
- Purpose can be stated as a problem, need or mission.
- Purpose can be interrogated using the five whys.
- A shared vision brings the outcome to life.
- No battle plan survives contact with the enemy.
- Create an adaptable schedule.
- Ask 'what can I get for my budget?' rather than 'how much will it cost?'
- Test key assumptions as quickly and cheaply as possible.

Prepare the Soil

> **Exercise**
>
> Think about your change. What could it mean to prepare the soil? Write down your thoughts before you read on.

A Personal Failure

A shade over 20 years ago, I joined a start-up management consultancy firm. The founding partners were well-known in the sector and had already secured a considerable level of funding. It was a fantastic opportunity for me, as it simultaneously hit three of my career targets: nimble start-up, investment banking and management consultancy.

I squeezed in because the founding partners believed that investment banking operations could learn from the way I had helped transform retail banking operations over the preceding five years. The firm's customer proposition brought five competencies to the table: strategy, risk management, operations, programme management and technology. I had experience of the last three of these, particularly programme management, although not of investment banking.

During my first year in the firm, I found myself as one of the thought-leaders in the embryonic programme management practice. I built a reputation as a curious, fast learner, and as a reliable hard worker. The business grew at a dizzying pace. When the annual reviews rolled around, I hoped my reputation would see me promoted from *principal consultant* to *managing principal*, just one level below partner.

Unfortunately, however, that didn't happen. The feedback was that I 'wasn't ready'. I wasn't too disappointed, because of my newness to the sector, which I assumed to be the main sticking point. In the meantime, I was getting well paid and the people in the firm were the best I had ever worked with, so I was happy to knuckle down for another year. During that year, I aimed to learn as much as I could about my new sector and I took on roles commensurate with being a managing principal. Next time round, promotion would be a no-brainer. Or so I thought.

Promotion decisions were arrived at by consensus. That was because the firm was project-based. It was, in theory, the leaders of the projects you worked on who evaluated your performance. Instead of a line manager, each person had a mentor, who was responsible for their personal and professional development. A mentor could participate in the promotion decision-making process as an advocate for their mentee, but their voice was one among many.

In practice, there was a meeting for each territory, facilitated by HR. The meeting considered each grade in turn. The goal was to rank everyone in that grade relative to each other in order to create a pecking order. The facilitator wrote each person's name on a Post-it. Then they asked for views on that person and sought a consensus that ranked them relative to those already discussed. Finally, the facilitator asked where to draw the promotion line.

The overall process looked like the picture below. In practice, however, the meeting considered each grade separately. When it reached the grade you were on, you left the meeting.

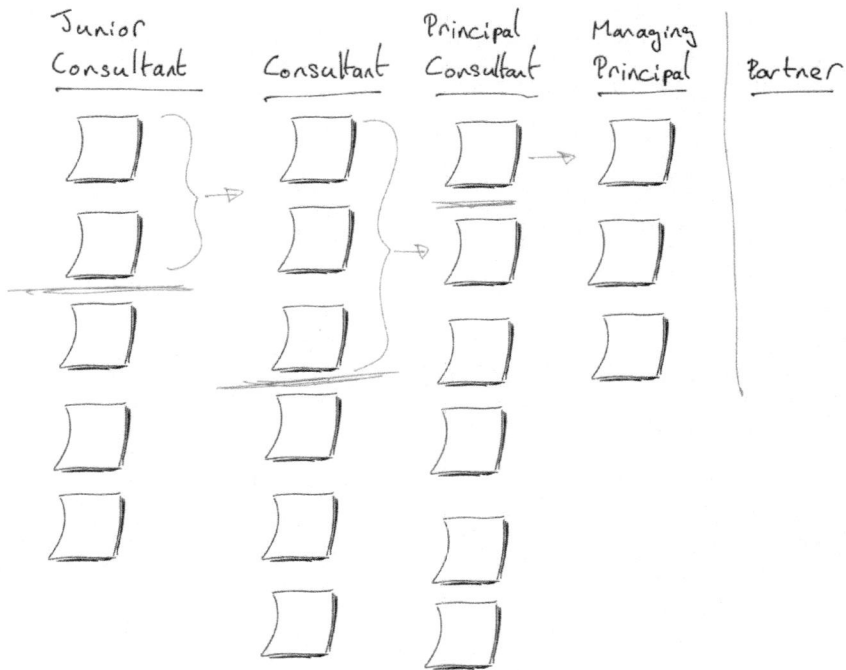

As you've probably guessed, I didn't get promoted. With hindsight, it's embarrassingly evident that I hadn't prepared the soil for the promotion ecosystem. I behaved as a mechanic and assumed my track record would speak for itself. I also thought that my mentor would be a powerful voice in my favour.

Unfortunately, not all voices in a meeting have equal influence. Some people command more respect than others. Sometimes someone is more influential than others because they are a type of person with whom others want to avoid conflict unless they feel strongly about the topic.

In this case, there was a partner whose nickname was 'The Prince of Darkness'. He was a difficult, confrontational individual who held grudges. In short, he was a bully, obsequious to those in power, but bullying towards everyone else. I got on with him fine until I opted to stick with an assignment I was learning from rather than a lead a mundane project for him. He never forgot or forgave.

Too late, I realised what I should have done to improve my chances. However, I wasn't keen to wait another year in order to find out. So, when an attractive opportunity presented itself a couple of months later, I was ready to leave, and did so.

Exercise

Write down what you think I could have done to prepare the soil, to get promoted? When you've done that, I'll tell you how I used my failure to help someone else succeed.

Prepare Well

When I met Mike, he was running a large division of a manufacturing company. He had been an outstanding achiever throughout his career. His progression seemed to occur naturally, without any additional effort on his part. He was one level below the main Board and had asked me to help him make the step up to join the Board.

My first question was: 'Who decides whether you join the Board?' He shook his head and laughed. He had never really thought about it. 'OK, how do I find out?', he asked.

'How do you think?', I replied.

I broke the silence that followed. 'Who do you think is the most influential decision-maker?'

'Obviously the CEO', he said, moving a little uncomfortably in his chair.

'You don't seem exactly keen to ask her?', I said.

'What if she tells me I am out of my mind?'

'Do you think she would say that?', I asked. 'And anyway, wouldn't it be good to hear it now rather than later?'

He was still hesitant, so I carried on. 'If you talk to her, you will achieve several things:

- You will find out quickly whether she can see you on the Board, at some point at least.
- You will have registered your ambition.
- If she indicates that you are not ready yet, you can ask what you need to do to close the gap between where you are now and where you want to get to.
- And if she advises you what you need to do to achieve it, you will potentially have recruited an influential mentor.
- You can ask her to identify the most influential decision-makers.'

'I'll do it', he said, as he stood up.

'Hang on', I said, 'who do you think are the other decision-makers?'

'Probably the rest of the Board', he said.

'All of them?'

'Well, I guess some are more interested than others. And some are more influential than others.'

'After the CEO, who do you think is most influential?'

'The Finance Director', he said without hesitation, 'but he is an ogre and has never been friendly towards me.'

'So, talk to him as soon as possible', I said.

'No way', said Mike, 'I'll leave him to last.'

A gardener doesn't plant a whole crop in untested soil and wait until the end of a season to discover that it has failed.

If it's a particular type of plant, a quick acidity test will determine whether the soil is suitable. If it's not, then the gardener will either have to plant elsewhere or try to modify the soil. The latter is always a long-term challenge because the acidity will naturally try to equalise with that of the surrounding soil.

In other words, tackle the most significant risks first. Whether it's personal or organisational change, I often see people doing the easy stuff first. They are almost hoping that the most worrying risks will evaporate over time.

I told Mike about the time I didn't get promoted. 'So, you're saying I should talk to the two most influential people first?', he said. I told him I couldn't tell him what to do. He needed to decide for himself. I could only share my experience.

The next time I met Mike, he was very animated. He opened up his laptop to show me something with which he was pleased. It was a spreadsheet in which he had scores against most of the Board members. Not only had he talked to the CEO and the Finance Director, but the feedback he received gave him the confidence to speak to the other Board members.

He told me he had asked each person to rate his suitability and readiness on a scale of one to five. Where a score fell below five, he asked what he would have to do to make it a five. But he didn't leave it there. He finished by asking Board members two direct questions:

- If I can demonstrate that I achieved what you suggested, will you support my promotion to the Board?
- Can I meet with you, say quarterly, to check whether I am on track?

Mike's analytical and direct approach may not be for everyone, but I sure could have done with it when I was failing to get promoted. I cross-checked what Mike had done versus Christopher Lloyd's advice to gardeners on how to prepare the soil. Lloyd says that the key things to do are:

- Aerate
- Enrich
- Dig deeper

Aerating, says Lloyd, helps drainage, lets earthworms move freely, and enables roots to spread and anchor. Enriching replaces nutrients to ensure that the soil is fertile. Dig deeper to find out what the earth is like below. If there is clay beneath, it will stop the roots penetrating, so they will dry out in summer.

I believe that Mike did all three of these when he did the rounds of the Board members. The effect of his conversations went beyond digging deeper in order to get information. He was aerating by making Board members aware of his ambition. And his questions about what he needed to accomplish enriched the conversation by making Board members think more deeply than their instinctive reaction to his stated ambition. He tilled the soil and made it fertile and ready for growth.

Christopher Lloyd's advice is equally applicable to organisational change. In the chapter 'Prune', I'll write about a substantial change programme that I inherited. The programme had an established monthly Steering Committee of senior people who knew each other well. A wise management consultant taught me to talk to the Committee's most influential members in advance of committee meetings if there was anything in the slightest contentious on the agenda. This was time-consuming, but avoided more time-consuming derailments.

The value of doing so was brought home to me in the second Steering Committee meeting. Before the meeting, we ran an idea past the Director of Operations. He was vehemently opposed to what we proposed, but we agreed to keep negotiating with him. When the item came up in a monthly meeting, he leaned forward and all heads turned in his direction, expecting fireworks.

I looked at him and said: 'Phil, I know we disagree on this, but we're continuing to talk about it, to find a workable solution?'

He leaned back, pleased to hear his disagreement acknowledged in public and said: 'Yes, absolutely.' Had we not discussed it with him in advance, I am sure he would have rolled a hand grenade on to the table and blown up the whole meeting, preventing us from discussing the many other items on the agenda.

But what of Mike's ambition to get on the Board? Well, he didn't get on the Board of that particular company. The CEO was chosen by the investors, a private equity firm, who wanted the CEO to turn Mike's company around so that they could sell it. The CEO was so impressed by Mike's approach to self-development that she recommended Mike to be one the private equity firm's cadre of potential CEOs. As a consequence, Mike was offered the role of Chief Operating Officer in a more prominent company, with a view to him taking over the top position.

Stakeholder Maps

If soil is the thing in which change is rooted and grows, for most of my work, that's people. By people I mean individuals, organisations and groups. All are equally important, but special care is needed with groups because they are not always formal, visible organisational units. Informal groups, bound together by common interests and identity, can be potent inhibitors or drivers of change.

It's really useful to draw the ecosystem of those who will be affected by a proposed change, together with those involved in making the change happen. I call this *a stakeholder map.* Below is an example of a project whose purpose was to help homeless people.

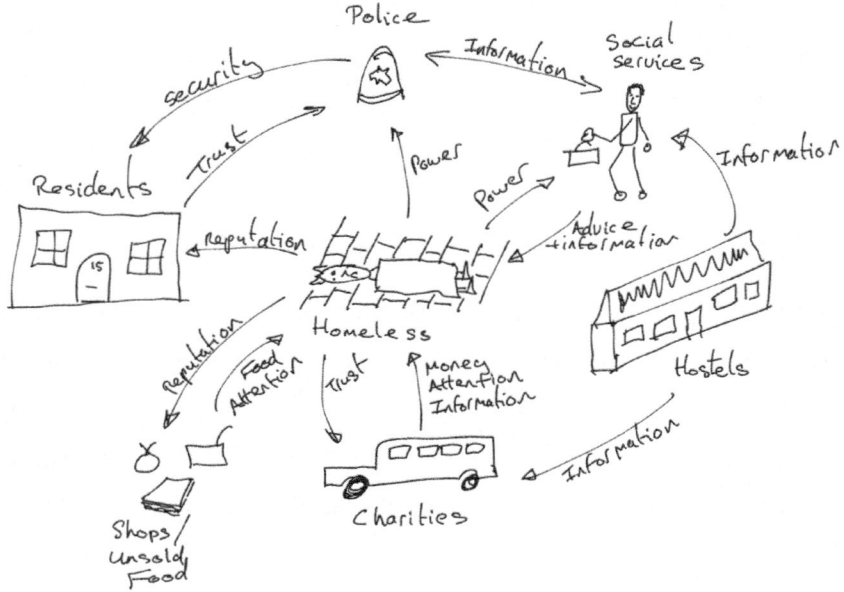

This picture represents the ecosystem before any change occurs. You know you want to change that ecosystem, but you don't yet know how.

A gardener thinks about what will grow in the soil *before* deciding what to plant. They ask themselves: what will thrive here? In contrast, a mechanic designs an ideal change and then worries about how the ecosystem needs to change to make it work.

Evaluate options for change based on what will thrive in your ecosystem rather than deciding on a change and then trying to shoehorn it in.

The picture above shows the essential stakeholders and the *value* that currently flows between then. If you prefer, you can think in terms of *benefits* flow rather than *value* flow. I prefer *value* because it implies a ratio of benefit to cost. This ratio is helpful when it comes to evaluating potential solutions.

A picture like this helps to identify interdependencies and explore unintended consequences that might ripple through the ecosystem. For a given option for change, you could ask: how will a stakeholder's flows of value change? It also helps to think about what is outside your control.

To draw this picture, I first placed a homeless person at the centre. I asked myself who would be affected by or involved in a change. As noted in the chapter 'Ecosystem Characteristics', this is better than making a linear list because it mirrors the way your mind works.

Sometimes I found myself labelling the connection as a flow of value as I went along. At other times, I had to think about the relationship and ask myself: what does this stakeholder get from this other stakeholder? There's no correct way of doing it. Nor is there a proper format for the finished picture. The thinking process is what's important.

If your change is an organisational one, then drawing this sort of picture, together as a team, is a great way to collaborate. Posting it on the wall for the duration of your change project makes it an open invitation for others to contribute.

If your change is a private, personal one, such as a career change, this type of picture is still a powerful way of exploring who else is involved and how they will be affected. You can keep the image in your back pocket or you can use it to get input from people you trust. Ask them: what have I forgotten?

And don't forget to consider the role of emotion. What do people currently feel? How, for example, does a homeless person or a resident feel? Only by doing so will you be able to evaluate the emotional impact of any given change.

Exercise

Draw a stakeholder map for your change. As you think about each stakeholder, think about what they currently feel and the assumptions and beliefs that underlie those feelings. Initially, this will be guesswork, but your next step will be to test those guesses by talking directly to those stakeholders in order to really understand and nourish your soil.

Key Points

- Identify individuals, groups and organisations whose support you will need for your change.
- Enrich the soil by having one-to-one conversations in order to understand their viewpoint.
- Ask for advice to get help and enlist support.
- Draw a picture to understand the ecosystem for your change.
- Pay attention to emotions and keep testing your assumptions.

Plant

Getting off to a Good Start

Robin, a friend of mine, has many qualities. He is charming, diplomatic and strategically astute. He loves starting new things and works incredibly hard to ensure there's a clear purpose and vision. He's also good at preparing the soil. Robin is not, however, fond of getting involved in the day-to-day detail of getting stuff done. He can do that detailed work, but prefers the big picture stuff.

Some time ago, Robin had networked his way into a role as Director for which he was perfectly suited. He worked in a financial services organisation with a history of public technology project failures. The most recent failure led to the departure of the CEO, who had been the project's figurehead.

Robin managed to meet with the incoming CEO before he had even taken up the role. By the time they met, he had spoken to several people who had seen the project failure at first hand. The problem, he told the new CEO, was that his new organisation lacked people who understood both their business and the technology upon which it relied. The consequence, he said, was a flawed technology strategy, with poor execution. Millions had been wasted on top-tier consultancies doing the wrong thing badly.

The solution, Robin told the CEO, was to recruit a cadre of senior people who understood both the business and the technology involved. Such a group, he argued, could act as the strategic bridge that could help deliver what the organisation needed most, inexpensively and with a low degree of risk. The CEO clearly thought it was worth a try because he hired Robin to set up and run the unit he had proposed.

The next 18 months were ones of drama-free refurbishment. The project that failed was supposed to replace a group of old systems. There was therefore a pent-up demand for changes to those old systems. This pent-up demand was efficiently addressed and delivered by a new technology leadership team, including Robin's strategic unit.

Delivering incremental change is not, however, that exciting for ambitious technologists. During the 18 months of refurbishment, the new IT leadership team discussed doing something more significant once the memory of failure had faded. From those discussions emerged a bold vision of how new technologies could transform the competitiveness of one of the organisation's products.

Robin prepared the soil brilliantly. He tested out ideas with critical influencers inside and outside the organisation, asking for advice and making them part of the creative process. Momentum gathered and the CEO, having spent his first two years restoring the organisation's reputation, was also ready for something bolder than business as usual. He gave Robin the green light to lead a project to deliver the vision.

Rather than run the project himself, Robin decided to take a step up and fulfil the role of the project sponsor. He wanted to use his energy to shift his group out of IT and make it the engine of business strategy, and to launch reputation-building initiatives.

To run the project on a day-to-day basis, Robin recruited Alan, someone who had worked for him in the past and whom he regarded as loyal and reliable. Unfortunately, the person he hired to plant and nurture the tender seedling was strong on process, but weak on content and people. This would be a problem because there were still plenty of sceptics, particularly in middle management, who were ready and willing to undermine the project. In gardening terms, while the soil had been well-prepared, the project had yet to put down solid roots as a basis for healthy growth.

Exercise

How would it have helped Robin if he had thought in terms of *planting*? What does it mean to plant well?

How to Plant Well

Christopher Lloyd sets out five steps for planting or transferring a plant:

- Soak root ball.
- Tease out roots.
- Create a hole large enough to take roots comfortably.
- Firm in.
- Water thoroughly.

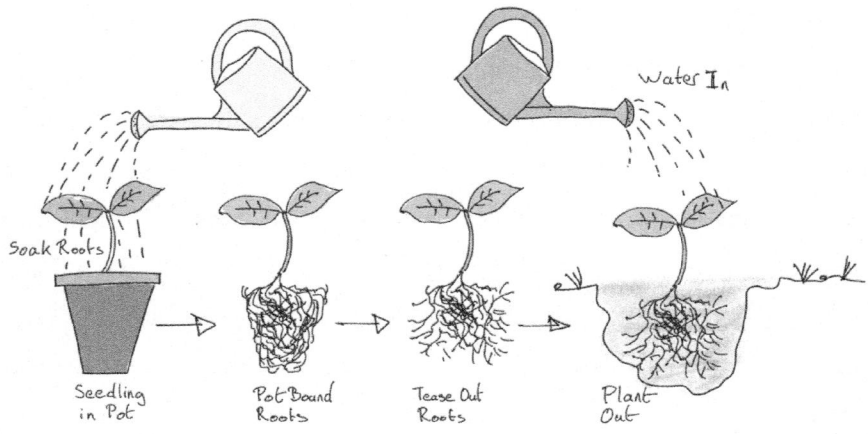

Whether it's a plant or project to effect your change, it's most vulnerable during the early stages of growth.

If you just put a young plant in the ground, walk away and assume it will prosper, your probability of success will be low.

In Robin's case, although the project had strong roots, they still needed to be teased out and secured within the rest of the organisation. This was a job that Alan, the Project Manager, was not equipped to do.

However, Alan was reluctant to take advice from anyone but Robin. A project of that size and industry-wide visibility was a big step up for Alan. He saw it as a career-defining moment. Consequently, he didn't want others to think he was unable to cope and ignored the advice of more seasoned heads on the team.

To compound the problem, Robin was rarely available when Alan hit a roadblock and needed support and advice. Snatched conversations took place along corridors as Robin marched between executive and client meetings. On one occasion, Alan found himself stranded at Heathrow Airport, with no money in his pockets, after he pursued Robin into an airport-bound taxi.

Robin's project isn't an extreme case. I have frequently seen leaders of substantial change projects hand over the day-to-day running to someone else and then stop paying close attention. Those leaders assume it's then sufficient to turn up for regular steering committee meetings, at which they behave like interested passengers rather than drivers.

If you want to harvest the benefits of your change, you need to stay intimately involved throughout, taking particular care during the early stages of growth. Think of your new projects, large or small, as tender seedlings that need to be protected and nurtured. Often it's less experienced members of the team who need to be nurtured. Had Robin taken the time to nurture Alan, through a coaching approach, both Alan and the project would have benefited.

Think about people you have recruited or teams you have been part of or perhaps created. Have they been plonked into the ground and expected to prosper? Or maybe you have taken on a new role. How are you going to ensure you get the start you need?

Let's do an exercise and then I'll tell you what happened to Robin's project.

Exercise

Think about what Christopher Lloyd's five steps to good planting might mean for your change. Don't forget that there is no right answer. The goal is simply to take your thoughts down paths that might otherwise remain unexplored.

Planting

I have skipped past an essential element of planting, which is whether to plant in light or shade. Some plants prosper in full sunlight, while others thrive in the shade, with many gradations in between. One way you might think about this in a work context is to equate light to the degree of attention something gets from above.

Robin's project survived its poor start, but it didn't thrive. It still puzzles me that he never realised this unless there was a visible crisis. As a plant, the project struggled to reach the light, like those leggy and weak plants you see on windowsills.

And it wasn't just the sponsor's attention that was needed. Robin had initially pulled together sufficient senior supporters who understood the project's strategic value. But when the project started to struggle, it required that director-level support in order to fend off the attack by sceptical middle managers. Alan didn't have Robin's direct connection to those senior supporters or the skill to coax them into battle.

The project didn't entirely die, but it was scaled back significantly when it became clear it wouldn't deliver the promised harvest. A strategic solution had turned into an expensive tactical solution and Robin's career in that organisation never really recovered.

But changes at work do not always benefit from being in full sun. Some benefit from being in a dark corner, in the shade of a big tree.

Does your change need slight or shade?

In 1982, Tom Peters and Robert Waterman wrote the first blockbuster management book, entitled *In Search of Excellence*[39]. It sold three million copies in its first four years and it shaped the thinking of a generation of business leaders. The book summarised the authors' research and aimed to uncover what excellent companies do in order to be successful. The conclusions were distilled into actionable insights that almost every organisation raced to emulate. The book's ideas and language are now so integrated into our thinking that it is difficult to appreciate how radical it was at the time.

One of the terms introduced was *skunkworks*. The authors argued that innovation thrived when it avoided the attention of formal management structures processes. Informal teams, often literally hidden in basements, used whatever resources they could beg, borrow or steal to pursue crazy ideas. Often those ideas would come to nothing. But sometimes they would break into the sunlight, as industry-changing innovations that are commercialised by the traditional organisation.

Peters and Waterman's anecdote-based insight has stood the test of time. In the 40 years that have elapsed since the book's publication, study after study has shown that conventional management structures and processes stifle innovation. They also find that limited resources create a wellspring of creativity. From books and articles on *corporate venturing* and *intrapreneurship*, through to Eric Reis' *The Lean Startup*[40], it's now the received wisdom that innovation prospers best in the shade.

There's no right answer. Like a gardener, you have to make an initial judgement and experiment to find out what works best for your unique circumstances. If you've followed the suggestions from the previous chapter, you will have a solid base on which to build.

Exercise

Build on the exercise given earlier in the chapter. Will your change benefit from light or shade at this stage of its life? But don't forget that there's a spectrum between shadow and sun.

Don't just take my analogy and equate light to attention. Perhaps it could mean something else in your context?

Key Points

- Preparing the soil is not enough to ensure a seedling will thrive.
- Ensure roots are going in the right direction and have space to spread.
- Ensure your change is firmly anchored.

- Ensure you continue to give it the right degree of attention.
- Will your change prosper best in light or shade, or something in between?

Prune

How I Learned to Garden

In my mid-thirties, my employer, a leading bank, paid for me to do an MBA at a leading UK business school. Before I went to business school, I had worked for most of my career in IT. The MBA was my opportunity to change direction and avoid being pigeonholed. When I returned from the MBA, I chose to join the bank's most significant business: retail banking.

My role was to be the apprentice to a highly regarded boss, who was running a significant business process reengineering programme. However, by the time I arrived to take up my role, my boss had moved on to run a more challenging programme. I had to step into his vacant shoes with immediate effect.

My briefing for the new role lasted little more than an hour. The man who would have been my boss explained that I had inherited a programme of 12 projects. Each had a significant IT component and an estimated budget. More importantly, each project had to deliver a per annum cost saving. My performance, he told me, would be judged on my ability to deliver the total cost saving for the programme. I went home and said to my wife: 'I think I'm in big trouble.'

There was a knot in my stomach when I arrived at the office the next day. I opened the door and walked into an open-plan office. Around 30 heads turned in my direction. Here was the hotshot MBA who was going to lead these seasoned retail bankers.

Before I had time to start physically shaking, or indeed sit down, a woman appeared. 'Don't worry', she said, with the slightest of French accents, 'I am Daphne from BCG, and I'm here to help you.' I was about to object when she said: 'I can bring you up to speed quickly and save you wading through all of that paperwork. Can I buy you a coffee?' It was an offer I couldn't refuse.

I later discovered that Daphne was my guardian angel: my minder and my tutor. The Boston Consulting Group (BCG) had convinced the bank's executives that they could save much money and improve customer service by 'redesigning its core processes'. It was something BCG's London office had turned into a speciality. The Group had an impressive track record and employed a bunch of tireless, super-smart people.

My programme was one of a number across different divisions of the bank, not just retail banking. Each programme manager, of which I was now one, had a senior BCG consultant attached to them full-time for the duration of the programme. These minders were supported by a pool of more junior consultants who guided the retail banking bank staff who had been seconded to make up the project teams.

Over coffee, Daphne told me she thought that at least half of the projects I had inherited were 'duds'. She said she had looked carefully at the projects' underlying assumptions and concluded they wouldn't deliver their estimated cost savings. She suggested I chair a project-by-project review, which she would structure for me.

At this point, I had no reason to trust Daphne's judgement. And I was puzzled by her implication that my predecessor had left me with a career-limiting time-bomb. I said I would think about the review idea, but resolved to talk to my predecessor about what she had said. He had offered to be 'available any time to help' and his judgement would surely be more aligned with the organisation's goals than an outside consultant.

He looked at me grimly. 'Well, everything was fine when I left it', he said. 'Was there anything else?' This from the guy who would have been my boss had he not been given a more important job to do, because of his stellar reputation for delivering complicated stuff. I was on my own.

Except, it turned out that I wasn't. There was Daphne. I didn't tell her what my predecessor said. I just parked my ego and asked whether she had thought about the form the reviews might take. She pulled out a sheet of paper with a flowchart on it, describing her proposed review process.

She explained that no-one senior cared about individual projects; they cared about the total amount of money the bank aimed to save by doing them. I had nothing to lose and everything to gain from setting up the reviews, so gave Daphne the green light.

As such, we reviewed each project with the project team members. And when it became apparent that I was genuinely listening, not only did they identify the duds, but they also started to suggest other projects that needed doing and would save money.

It was BCG who taught me how to garden. I learned that the roots of successful projects are people and relationships, not processes, procedures and charts (although these do have their place). BCG made it easy to learn from them. Their ethos was to make their clients, not themselves, look good. Thus, feedback felt like coaching rather than criticism or challenge.

I came to understand that Daphne's measure of success was my visible success, without her having to step out of the shadows,

So we started pruning, existing projects in order to create space for new growth. If a project wasn't going to yield the expected harvest, I stopped it immediately and reassigned the team to investigate new opportunities.

This ruthless pruning caused consternation amongst my erstwhile colleagues in IT. They had lined up people to work on the projects and were often keen to try out their latest technology toys. The head of development came to see me to tell me that I was a loose cannon and couldn't just change my mind on a whim.

'Are you telling me', I asked, 'you want me to tell the director of retail banking that we are going to pursue half a dozen projects that will lose the bank money so that we don't inconvenience our IT department?' This was a harsh but fair statement.

After a long pause, barely containing his irritation, he said: 'We always said those projects would be expensive and risky. No-one wanted to listen. If your goal is to save money, there are loads of other projects you could do!'

'Now that', I said, 'is something I would like to hear about.' Daphne gave me a congratulatory kick under the table. It had been a tense encounter and I'm pretty sure my desire to hear about other opportunities rang hollow. But the next day I called him. I asked whether some of the IT people, freed up from the cancelled projects, could co-locate with my teams for three months in order to identify and initiate new projects.

To this day, I don't know whether my suggestion was mischievous bluff-calling or a moment of inspiration. However, I am certain that it was one of the smartest things I did on that programme. After a couple of days to think about it, he agreed to a co-location experiment.

The joint retail banking and IT teams started the new week with a series of workshops. Many IT-dependent changes that the bankers assumed to be difficult turned out to be simple, and vice versa. Also, the IT people had an excellent understanding of the operational processes because the IT systems had those same processes embedded within them.

Our pruning exercise didn't just replace one project with another; it increased the projected cost savings. We were also vigilant and not afraid to prune new growth as well as old. Assumptions made early on can turn out to be wrong, or conditions may change that then invalidate those assumptions. Pruning wasn't a one-off exercise. It was an ongoing discipline.

This is just like a real garden. Rose bushes, for example, benefit from regular pruning in order to stay healthy and flower throughout the spring and summer. The same is true for personal and organisational projects. Christopher Lloyd offers the following pruning advice:

- Remove old branches that have done their job.
- Contain plants that are too vigorous for their location.
- Thin out to let in air and light.
- Develop the desired shape.
- Timing depends on the type of plant and the conditions for growth.

In short:

A gardener removes old redundant growth, when
appropriate, to create space for new, more vibrant
growth to come through and bear fruit.

Some plants, such as roses, benefit from brutal pruning. But for some other plants, fruit comes only from existing rather than new growth. So don't assume you should prune out anything old, as it may still be adding much value.

Although the example above was for a sizeable organisational programme, the pruning analogy is as equally applicable to career change, as I will illustrate in the next section. How often have you dissipated your energy across many things, making no major progress on any single one of them? Maybe it is time for some pruning?

Exercise

Think about your change and ask:
- Would it benefit from some pruning?
- What would be the purpose of that pruning?
- When would be the best time to do it?

Write down your thoughts.

Pruning Your Resumé

When I first read Christopher Lloyd's pruning tips, I was particularly struck by *thinning out to let in air and light*. If I hadn't seen his list, I wouldn't have thought of it. But the more I think about it, the more I realise what a powerful analogy it provides.

In a real garden, to remove parts of a plant that are not going to yield fruit, so that energy goes towards new growth, is obvious common sense. But pruning away healthy growth is more challenging to come to terms with. Yet this is sometimes what you need to do, to enable a plant to prosper.

In the spring, it's a joy to see early flowers on the rose bushes, brightening the garden after the grey of winter. Often, however, these flowers are on stems that have suddenly shot up, high above the rest of the rose bush, shading the lower parts and other smaller plants.

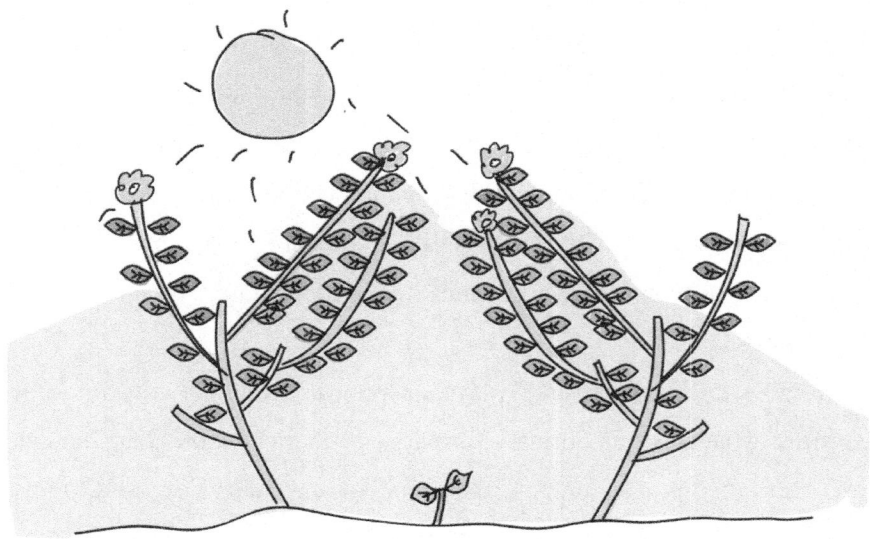

Although I know I should prune back these spurts of growth for the long-term health of the bush, I have a mental tussle because it means losing those beautiful flowers that have worked so hard to be there. Work throws up similar challenges.

A client who asked me to help her change her career direction wanted me to review her resumé. The document she sent me turned out to be the epitome of something that needed more air and light. She told me she had worked hard on the version she sent to me, but thought it might need a few tweaks.

When I saw it, my heart sank. It was just over three pages, with a chronological list of responsibilities, described in long sentences and little or no white space. Next came a list of qualifications that went back to her schooldays. Try as I might, I couldn't get past the first few densely typed lines. Her resumé was a poor representation of the bright and curious woman to whom I enjoyed talking.

I asked her to think about the role she wanted her resumé to play in her job search. She had already come around to the idea that her best option was a targeted networking strategy. Rather than apply for advertised jobs, with hundreds of applicants, she would make direct contact with individuals in organisations she admired. She would then try to get an informal meeting, ideally over coffee, and impress them by exploring their issues and needs. The central idea is that people hire people they like. And people like those people who demonstrate genuine curiosity about them and their organisation.

In this strategy, the resumé plays a supporting role, not a lead role. It confirms what was said during informal conversations rather than being a key that attempts to unlock the door to an interview. And, most importantly, it highlights what an individual has achieved, not the roles they have held.

I knew from what she had told me that she had already put a lot of effort into the version of the resumé she had shared with me. So instead of asking her to change the actual resumé, I asked her to write a bullet-pointed list of achievement that could be considered for inclusion as an *experiment.*

What she produced was a list of roles and responsibilities. It wasn't a list of achievements, but at least it was more readable than the previous roles and responsibilities section. Extraneous words had been removed and it had plenty of space, which made it easier on the eye. I sensed the door was open to change.

I knew the achievements section is the most difficult one to get right, but it is also the most important, so I persisted. She was disconsolate. 'I don't have any "wow!" achievements', she said.

Your achievements don't have to make people say 'wow!', I told her. You just want to show what you have achieved and therefore the value you can add in future. I asked her to think about what she had described as role responsibilities. I suggested that she should ask herself what changed, or what target was met, as a consequence of her being in the role; team achievements could also be described, but it was important for her to explain what she did personally as part of the team.

Three days later, she sent me a genuinely impressive list of achievements. I asked her to see what it would look like if she included them at the top of her resumé and she agreed. In the next iteration she sent me, she had also pruned the roles and responsibilities section to only four things: who, what, where and when.

There were just two things left to do. First, to add a short bullet-pointed list of key skills. Second, to prune her profile summary, to strip out the non-differentiating waffle and make the summary an overview of her achievements, plus one final sentence saying what she was seeking.

She was concerned that the summary profile paragraph duplicated the achievements section that followed. I suggested she think of it as a newspaper. The opening paragraph should be just enough to make the reader read on.

By the end of four iterations, she had just two impressive pages, with lots of white space, making her resumé easy on the eye.

It had been very much a gardening exercise. A series of pruning experiments introduced air and light. After each iteration, she checked the overall shape in order to create something that fitted into the target space.

I asked her to place the old and new resumés side by side, and she just started laughing. Seeing the revised version, she was embarrassed by the earlier version.

There is something I omitted from this anecdote. After an initial flurry of emails and Skype calls with my client, there was a period of about two weeks when she stopped communicating with me. It turned out that the seemingly simple task of revising her resumé had caused her to reflect deeply on how she saw herself. Her work identity was previously a long list of roles and responsibilities. However, pruning it back to just achievements and skills told a different story about her. And our identities, some argue, are no more than the stories we tell ourselves.

Her new story was not one of technical competence, but rather one of using personal qualities, such as curiosity, persistence and charm, to overcome difficult challenges in order to achieve results. Her new story widened her horizon of career possibilities.

I am going to finish this chapter with an exercise that focuses on personal growth and happiness.

Over time every one of us acquires assumptions, beliefs and habits that shape our behaviour. In the main, we do so without realising it. That's not a bad thing. Evolution has designed us to run on autopilot as much as possible, freeing our conscious minds to deal with potentially threatening changes in our environment.

For example, when you sit down in a car, you probably put on a seatbelt, without much conscious thought. It's a habit grounded in the belief that you will be safer if you wear a seatbelt. Underlying that belief is the assumption that the seatbelt will stop your head from hitting the windscreen if the car is in a collision. Most people believe it's a positive habit to have.

However, we also acquire assumptions, beliefs and habits that hold us back in some way. We extrapolate a handful of experiences into a general truth. In childhood, for example, we come to believe that we are good or bad at mathematics, sport or art. These classic examples often persist throughout our lives.

Positive beliefs can make us confident and brave. Negative beliefs often stop us from even attempting something. I'll talk more about this topic in the chapter 'Ensure Good Health' when I discuss a Growth Mindset versus a Fixed Mindset. But you don't have to wait until then to get pruning.

You'll probably be more aware of the assumptions, beliefs and habits that originated in childhood, because of their lifelong impact. But we continue to acquire new assumptions, beliefs and habits in adulthood. So, from time to time, it pays to stop and prune out those that are self-limiting. Here's a simple exercise to help you do that.

Exercise

Close your eyes and imagine yourself twelve months ago. What can you see, hear and feel? Now contrast that with now and ask yourself three questions:

- How have my *assumptions* about the world changed?
- What *beliefs* have I acquired or thrown away?
- What *habits* have I gained or lost?

For each question, write down a list of answers.

Now consider each item, ask yourself whether it has a positive or negative impact on your life? If it's an assumption, ask yourself, "am I sure?" and "how can I test it?" If it's a belief, dig out the underlying assumptions and test them.

Some of those assumptions and beliefs will probably be about your capabilities and qualities. If that's the case, then seek feedback from people you trust, to check whether your assumptions and beliefs are correct. We are rarely able to see ourselves as others see us!

If it's a habit that you want to prune out, identify what triggers it. Commit to re-purpose that trigger to do something else instead. It sounds ridiculously simple, but it works. Initially, you'll often miss the trigger and fall into the old habit. But when you realise later that you've missed the trigger, don't criticise yourself. The moments of awareness, after the fact, will gradually programme your unconscious mind to adopt a different pattern.

Key Points

- Focus on the overall health of your change.
- Remove anything that will not contribute to your desired outcome.
- Don't waste energy on growth that will not yield fruit.
- Don't allow what's important to be crowded out.
- If you are going to prune, consider when to do so – don't do it impulsively.
- Less is often more.

Weed

A Plant in the Wrong Place

A weed is not a particular type of plant that will always be unwanted, no matter where it grows.

A weed is a plant in the wrong place.

Grass is one of the most persistent weeds in our herb garden. It's vigorous and, if left to grow, will crowd out the herbs, stealing light and nutrients. But in our lawn area, grass is exactly what we want to grow.

In our flower garden we have a lot of self-sowing annuals (plants that distribute their seeds before dying off at the end of the year). Some plants, such as foxgloves, pop up in unexpected places the following year, their seeds having been carried on the wind. If I spot them early enough, I relocate them to somewhere else, where they will look and thrive better.

Weeding is different from pruning. Pruning trims back an established plant, usually a large one, to improve its prospects in the medium to long term. In contrast, weeding is the complete removal of a plant, preferably before it has had time to establish itself. Sometimes, a bed gets neglected and overgrown with weeds, necessitating a clear-out.

Weeds at work can take on a variety of forms, such as commitments and people. This might sound like a harsh way to describe a person, but let me illustrate what I mean by using myself as an example.

Look What Blew in

By the autumn of 2005, I had moved into freelance work and my track record ensured I wasn't short of work. I was in the enviable position of being able to choose which assignments I took. I only worked on interesting things and with people I liked.

Then something came along that changed my mind. A recruiter called me and said he had been asked to talk to me by someone I knew in one of the world's largest management consultancies.

Before I could finish my polite no thank you, the recruiter blurted out the name of his client and made me pause. The client and I had both worked at the start-up consultancy, where I had had so much fun. We had never worked on anything together, but knew each other from around the office. He was even more counter-cultural to the big firm than me. So I listened a little longer and agreed to meet my ex-colleague for an informal coffee.

We met in plush offices, in a prime location in London. 'I bet you're surprised to find me in a place like this?', he said. I nodded in agreement. 'And I bet you're surprised I am asking you to join me?', he continued. I nodded in agreement. My objection defused, I sat back and listened.

He told me he had joined the firm by accident after doing some freelance work for one of the partners. He and the partner hit it off, and the partner had asked him to join the firm to build an agile investment banking 'advisory' practice. He had warned the partner that it would mean hiring people who were a bit different from what they were used to. The partner said it sounded like fun and hired my ex-colleague on a generous salary.

After my ex-colleague convinced me he was deliberately seeking counter-cultural recruits, he offered me a salary that matched my freelancing income. And then came a big carrot. I would join on a 'fast track' to the position of partner.

He explained that where we used to work, *partner* was just a job title. However, partners in this firm were genuine legal partners. They ran their own profit centres, with a high degree of autonomy. The firm was effectively a federation of partners. And in that model, mavericks were welcomed as long as they made money – just as they were in investment banking.

My ego got the better of me. I thought about the buzz of creating a new consulting business, using the resources of a large global firm. I could put everything I had learned from the Boston Consulting Group and from the start-up consultancy into practice. The next day, I accepted his offer.

Two things happened between my acceptance and my arrival. First, the partner running the 'practice' I was to join moved on to set up a new practice and had taken my ex-colleague with him. Second, a new partner had arrived from another firm to take over the practice I had now joined. He brought with him a bunch of people he trusted, most of whom specialised in the insurance sector. The new partner and his senior acolytes had no interest in building an investment banking practice. They wanted to build an insurance practice, similar to what they had just left, except much bigger.

The ex-colleague who had coaxed me to join in the first place told me that the new partner wasn't 'a people person'. Not only was this true, but he also seemed to revel in this macho reputation. He vetoed proposals for team-building exercises and took no interest in personal development.

I responded to my new environment by doing my utmost to try to make things work. I networked like crazy within the firm, across different specialities and geographies. I tried to hook up with others who might be interested in building an investment banking advisory business.

With hindsight, I can see that we simply didn't fit the new partner's vision. He wanted less expensive, more junior people, with insurance experience. I was a weed in his garden.

I have seen similar things happen with some of my business school mentees, all of whom are highly competent and confident executives. They joined large organisations that, after a honeymoon period, seemed to set about convincing their recruits that they weren't satisfactory. The more the recruits tried to make things work and failed, the more their confidence was eroded.

It's difficult to realise when you are plant in the wrong place rather than being a *bad* plant. If you've been successful in the past, you will be used to taking on new challenges, struggling at times but ultimately thriving. So when you encounter a new difficulty, you persist and try to make things work. I have seen people stay for years in an organisation where they don't fit, stagnating and complaining. It helps if you have a critical friend who can help you think things through. A mentor is ideal.

Knowing about weeds should also make you more compassionate towards talented individuals who find themselves in the wrong place. For example, you may recruit someone into your organisation, but they have trouble thriving. Or maybe you partner with someone on a venture, but it doesn't seem to be working. They may be a talented individual, but it's just not a good fit. If that happens, think about how you would feel if you were them.

They will also know it's not working, so have an open discussion about it. And if they turn out to be a weed, help relocate them to somewhere they will thrive, without denting their sense of self-worth.

Commitment Weeds

Commitments can also turn out to be weeds, such as a project or some activity that interferes with your vision. A few years ago, I made a volunteering commitment that blew into my work garden.

I had an appointment at a local medical service. When I went into the small waiting room, there was only one other person present. She was seated behind a table at the end of the room. On the table were stacks of leaflets.

Like a lot of shy people, I'll often feel a compulsion to fill what I perceive to be awkward silences. So I asked her why she was there. By the end of the conversation, I had volunteered to attend a quarterly meeting, the purpose of which was to help the medical service stay connected to the needs of its customers.

A quarterly meeting didn't feel like a big commitment. But my desire to do the job well meant that this small commitment led to further duties. There were papers to read, subgroups and regional meetings. I came to enjoy the role less and less, but I couldn't shake the notion that the point of doing it was to be of help, not to enjoy myself. So I stuck with it, increasingly resentful of the time it took up. It was a weed in my garden.

However, recently, I got rid of the weed with a clear conscience. First, more than enough new volunteers joined, such that no-one would miss my departure. Second, I volunteered for a couple of different organisations and fell in love with the roles. It was possible to help others and be happy!

Weed out commitments that don't bring you joy.

Exercise

Have you made a commitment or a project that drains your emotional energy? Is there a way you could extract yourself without letting someone down? Your physical, mental and emotional resources are limited. Think hard about how you use them.

Now think about your change:
- Are there any weeds that interfere with your purpose and vision?
- Are they mature or at an early stage?
- How are you going to address them?

Key Points

- A weed is a plant in the wrong place, not a bad plant.
- Being in the wrong place doesn't mean an individual is any less valuable.

- Don't blame them for being in the wrong place.
- Treat people (including yourself) with compassion if they are in the wrong place.
- Help them relocate them to where they will be welcome and thrive.
- Beware of taking on commitments that are not consistent with your vision or drain your energy.

Water

Water Regularly

In 2002 I joined a financial derivatives exchange as a *programme manager*. Before I arrived, my new boss told me he wanted to ease me in gently with some small projects in order to get to know the organisation. However, on the day I arrived, he told me circumstances had changed. I would be immediately responsible for a programme to establish a new electronic derivatives exchange in Tokyo. He also told me not to worry because it was all pretty much under control.

The organisation I joined had decided to sell its technology platform to other exchanges. To do this, it had turned its IT department into a business within a business, named 'Market Solutions'. It had its own management functions, such as sales and marketing, and had its own managing director.

Its first big sale – of a full-blown exchange – was the programme I inherited when I arrived. We would be responsible for supplying and installing the exchange software, and for training the client staff how to use it. Regulation meant that the software had to run on equipment within Japan, so we had a Japanese technology partner. Our partner, a large Japanese company, would be responsible for the technical operations and for developing a back-office component of the overall solution.

On the afternoon of my first day, the Managing Director asked to see me. He just returned from Japan. He pulled a scrap of handwritten paper out of his pocket.

'The client CEO', he said, 'is unhappy and worried.' He paused for 'effect'. 'I am unhappy and worried.' He proceeded to read out the list of 'major' issues that he had noted down during his visit. Then he asked me what I was going to do about it.

I explained it was my very first day and I needed a bit of time to understand what was going on, so he gave me until Friday afternoon to come up with some answers. I made a copy of his list and scurried around for answers. It turned out that the project had been crawling along for six months, with two people almost permanently in Tokyo. One was a project manager and the other a *business analyst*. Both were *associates*. This means that they were not employees, but were trusted contractors, well-known to my new organisation, from previous assignments.

Getting hold of either of them for a telephone call proved to be surprisingly tricky. There is a nine-hour time difference between London and Tokyo, but I got the sense they were being evasive, in spite of me being their new boss – or perhaps because of it?

I finally caught up with the Project Manager on Thursday. The day before I sent him the list of issues I had compiled so far, including those from the Managing Director. The Project Manager explained to me how most of the issues were due to the client Project Manager, who was 'an incompetent clown'. He added that our Managing Director was a bit volatile and was probably overreacting.

I was anxious as I went into the meeting with the Managing Director. All I had to offer was a structured list of issues that I had put into a spreadsheet database. The list showed: when the issue was raised, who raised it, a target date for resolution and who was responsible for that resolution – basic project management practice. At this stage, I was the default owner of every single issue.

To my amazement, the Managing Director was delighted. I had turned his scrap of paper into something that someone else (me) would worry about on his behalf. He waved my printed list in the air, showing it to other people, saying how great it was. I was a bit embarrassed by his effusiveness, but I was mightily relieved to end my first week on a positive note.

The Managing Director requested that we have a weekly meeting to review progress, and I spent most of the next week trying to understand the issues and find out how to address them. Gradually, as I found my way around the organisation, the issues came under control, with people identified as being responsible for resolution, with realistic target dates.

However, about a month after my first meeting with the Managing Director, he called me in on a Monday. He had been to Tokyo. He told me he was unhappy and worried again, as was the client CEO.

I left his office and booked a ticket for my first trip to Tokyo. I was on the cusp of a valuable lesson. If I had my time over again, I would have visited as soon as possible, preferably during my first week. However, other things in my life meant I wasn't keen to spend a great deal of time in Tokyo. Also, I liked to think of myself as an enlightened boss, who wanted to give our Tokyo-based Project Manager the freedom to do his job without micro-management from me.

The Managing Director was delighted to hear I was going. 'I've worked in Japan a lot', he told me. 'And there are a few things you need to understand.'

First, the most critical thing to the Japanese businessperson is relationships. You need to spend time with people, especially outside work, to gain their trust.

Second, when a person speaks, be it you or them, that person is speaking on behalf of the whole company. This makes them reluctant to talk about things unless they have consulted widely.

Third, the presence of someone senior demonstrates seriousness. Later on, I had the experience of our client's chairman sleeping through a steering committee meeting. In the Japanese business culture, this was the opposite of showing disrespect. His presence sent an important message.

Those three pieces of advice turned out to be vital to the programme's success. On my first trip to Tokyo, I did much listening and much socialising. I took the first steps towards establishing formal relationships with the client and the Japanese partners.

When I met our onsite Project Manager, he reiterated that the stream of issues going back to London would dry up if we could persuade our client to get a more competent client Project Manager. The more I listened to his diagnosis of the problem, the less convinced I became. What did he do out here, I wondered? Perhaps I needed to do some weeding?

Later on, after I returned from dinner with our client and Japanese technology partner, I spotted the Business Analyst in the bar of the hotel. I asked if I we could chat and it was obvious he was keen to talk one-to-one. Before I left London, some people warned me that he was 'a slippery customer who had gone native. He cares more about the client's interests than ours'.

It turned out that this role of business analyst concealed a more interesting individual than had seemed the case at first glance. He had previously been a salaried employee in our organisation and was one of the key people who developed the software we were now selling. He understood the software platform inside and out, and had a terrific understanding of how the market operated, having been there since the beginning of the electronic market. As I found out later, he was also a good listener and had considerable charm.

He explained to me that many of the issues arose from the software platform. It had grown organically and was not designed to be packaged and sold as a shrink-wrapped product. Over the years, the platform acquired foibles that our exchange operations team chose to work around rather than pay to get fixed. The operational procedures assumed that staff knew not to do the equivalent of going straight from fifth to reverse in a geared car, even though it was mechanically possible.

However, Japanese business dictates that technology should prevent individuals from making stupid mistakes. A good car design should prevent it going from fifth gear into reverse.

Also, Japanese attention to detail is exceptionally close. The client team spotted things that didn't work as they were supposed to, according to the somewhat scant documentation, and they would raise an issue. On more than one occasion, our team in London didn't know how something worked, particularly for complex calculations embedded in the software long ago. In those instances, the client documented how they thought it should work and asked us to sign it off! Then, of course, we had to ensure that this was indeed how it worked, or else it would be yet another issue.

As a consequence, the Business Analyst was sending a constant stream of technical queries and issues back to London. The team in London was dismissive. If it was good enough for London, it should be good enough for Tokyo. Stop complaining and get on with it, they said. However, the Business Analyst knew that this was not acceptable to the Japanese client and it brought him into conflict with London, as he persisted doggedly in getting a satisfactory answer.

On top of the software issues, our London exchange operations staff were not helpful towards our client or our people on site. *Market Operations* was not part of the *Market Solutions* business and had not been in favour of the selling the platform in the first place,

At that stage, I had no idea whether the Business Analyst's assessment was accurate or self-serving. It was clear, however, that the client loved him. Perhaps he was a weed in London but not in Tokyo?

A couple of weeks after my trip, news of client unhappiness started to filter back to me once again. I tried resolving the issues through telephone conversations and conference calls, getting involved in low-level detail where necessary, but I sensed the client's unease.

It dawned on me that someone senior needed to *water the relationship* regularly, face to face. As our *programme manager*, that was my job. I resolved to visit Tokyo every four weeks, whether or not there was a specific reason to go. The purpose of the trips was to be present and listen in order to keep the relationship healthy.

Even great relationships will die unless you water them regularly.

Around the same time, the on-site Project Manager and the Business Analyst were back in London for a week. I spoke to each of them alone. The Project Manager told me he felt frustrated and undermined by my active involvement. He told me the programme didn't need both of us. I was inclined to agree, but I wasn't going anywhere. We terminated his contract and he never went back to Tokyo.

When I spoke to the Business Analyst, I asked him if he'd be interested in a more general relationship management role based in Tokyo. It was essentially formalising what he had already been doing, but with more freedom and more authority. I knew he loved Japan and he agreed without hesitation. This was a massive relief for me.

We agreed that, initially, I would keep an eye on his communication with the London team. This allowed me to determine whether he or the client was being unreasonable, the latter being what London had implied in earlier conversations.

It became apparent pretty quickly that he wasn't unreasonable. The members of the team in London were defensive because of the gaps in their knowledge. Calculations and rules had been programmed into the system long ago and were undocumented. To answer how something worked meant getting someone to try to read some ancient code. It was embarrassing. Their dismissive stance was borne out of a fear of looking stupid

I needed to find a way to tease out the roots. Over the next couple of months, we flew members of both the Market Solutions and Market Operations teams from London over to Tokyo, on some pretext or other, to meet the client team and our Japanese partners. The London team were amazed at how well our client and partners understood our platform, but, above all, our teams were bowled over by the hospitality they received in Japan. We all fell in love with Japan, its people and its food.

Subsequently, when a query arrived in London with a Japanese name attached, it was from someone with whom they had shared many beers and some fantastic food. There would still be groans at the level of detail, but now this was understood and accepted with good grace. Over the months that followed this first visit, I received a lot of requests from members of our teams to visit Tokyo in order to resolve some vague technical or operational query that could only be done face to face. The relationships needed to be watered at multiple levels, so I agreed to most requests, as long as there was sufficient slack in my budget.

There was one last part of the cultivation process that helped make the programme successful, but I'll return to this in the chapter 'Ensure Good Health'.

Irrigation

When I was going up, we mostly lived in high-rise housing, in which the flats usually had tiny balconies. From these small spaces, my dad produced so many tomatoes that we had to give a lot of them away.

He planted in wooden boxes that he brought home from his work in the docks and fed them with his special liquid fertiliser recipe, based on horse manure provided by the rag-and-bone men who used to tour our area in those days.

Indoors, every windowsill had something growing on it. Shoots grew from orange pips and lemon pips that were never likely to bear fruit, but it didn't stop my dad trying. Indoors or outdoors, he checked his plants every single day and nurtured them with love. I never took any interest in this.

When my wife and I moved out to the suburbs, long after my dad died, the enormous garden of our new home was one of its main attractions. By this point, I was a brilliant theoretical gardener. I visited my mum every

Friday evening and we used to watch *Gardeners' World* with Geoff Hamilton. 'Don't forget to tease out the roots!', we would shout at the television in unison.

So, when it came to my new garden, I was ready. Vegetables and tomatoes were top of my agenda. I created some raised beds halfway down the garden and chose the soil, compost and plants with great care. At the end of a long day of planting, I sat on the grass and admired the beautiful sight of the new beds, their dark soil and the vivid green seedlings, ready to do their work.

Unfortunately, however, the beds were out of sight of the house, and my commute to work meant that I was out for 12 hours every weekday. At first, I would water the beds regularly. But work became more demanding and I'd arrive home tired and distracted. The plants, upon which I lavished so much care at the planting stage, did not prosper.

I thought about my dad and the next year I resolved not to let the same thing happen again. But sadly it did. 'Out of sight, out of mind', my mum said when she visited that summer. Ouch! 'What about one of Geoff's leaky pipes?', she added in flash of brilliant insight.

The next year, I installed an irrigation system. This is a grand title for a few hoses with holes in the sides that provide a slow, steady drip of water, adjacent to the plants. It's a surprisingly economical use of water, especially when paired with a timer. The next year we had a bumper crop, particularly of tomatoes, which brought us great joy.

I love starting new projects, often with childish enthusiasm. But sometimes, once those projects are underway, I can get distracted by new things, just like my friend Robin who I mentioned in the previous chapter 'Plant'. It was a weakness that, at one time, nearly cost me my job.

When I was working in banking, I was running a programme with a boss whose mantra was 'let me know if you need any help, otherwise I'll leave you to get on with it'.

After a few months, however, I had a change of boss and my new boss instituted weekly one-on-one progress review meetings. Initially, he used to ask me whether I had any issues, and I used to respond that everything was fine and under control. I assumed that he trusted me, as had the previous boss, and that if I needed help, I'd ask for it.

With hindsight, this was incredible naivety on my part. As far as my new boss was concerned, I was, as he would tell me later, 'green as grass'. Not only did he have no reason to trust my judgement, as I was to learn, but he was also like my dad, always vigilant, checking for healthy growth and on the look-out for pests and diseases.

I came to dread those weekly meetings. He would sit leaning forward across a small round table in his office, underneath which his foot seemed to be continually twitching, as he battered me with a constant stream of questions. It was exhausting and demoralising.

Things came to a head one Friday evening at 8 pm in a tall office block overlooking London. He had worn me down and my confidence had wilted.

'Look', I said to him, 'I'm not sure whether you want me to do this job.' I had a knot in my stomach. Quitting this job was likely to be terminal for my career within that organisation and perhaps my reputation outside it.

After a long pause, he said: 'The thing is Gary, there must be loads of issues. If they're not on the table, then they're in the closet.'

What he said was gold dust. Not only did it help to resolve the conflict that had built up with my boss, but it was a lesson that served me well for every other project and programme I have run since then. I cannot count how many times I quoted his phrase about issues in the closet to people who worked for me.

'Of course,' I told my boss, 'there are issues and lots of them. There are also assumptions and risks.'

'Well, I'd like to see them', he said sceptically.

I am relieved to report that his scepticism was ill-founded. Aware of my 'out of sight, out of mind' weakness, I had installed an irrigation system.

Each project within the programme had a log of issues, risks and assumptions. Each item had a designated owner, the action to resolve it, the person responsible for the action and the target date for completion.

This was standard project management stuff, but rarely, in my experience, is it done with the rigour and attention it needs, particularly assumptions and risk, which are often two sides of the same coin.

The logs were reviewed weekly by the project managers and their teams, and I often sat in on those reviews, unannounced. If I didn't have time to sit in, I would read the logs on the train home.

The next day, I turned up to meet my boss with page after page of issues, risks and assumptions, printed raw from the logs. He picked up the pile of paper, gradually leaning backwards and smiling as he read through them. Now and then, something caught his eye and he asked me about it.

'See, I knew they were there', he said, delighted, 'but I needed to know that you knew they were there and you are managing them.' It was a turning point in our relationship. Someone who had felt like an enemy became my most prominent advocate when future work opportunities arose.

Now you might be like that boss, or my dad, with fantastic natural attention to detail and thus constantly vigilant. But even so, be aware you can be distracted by other things that seem urgent and crowd out the time you need for your medium-term and long-term goals. Or you might be more like me – you love new ideas, concepts and starting new projects, but sometimes you lack the diligence needed to make them bear fruit.

Either way, think about your change and how you are going to ensure it receives the regular water of your attention. Since I became aware of my inherent weakness in this regard, I have worked hard on this aspect of work, to the point that many people think it is one of my strengths.

Exercise

Think about your change and write down what you need to do to water it regularly.

Watering Your Good Seeds

In this section, I want to share some Buddhist wisdom that talks explicitly about watering and is particularly relevant to the relationships you form at work and your own mental health.

Zen Master Thich Nhat Hanh, the founder of the *Engaged Buddhism* movement, frequently uses gardening metaphors, similes and analogies. One of these is about watering the seeds of consciousness[41].

According to his teaching, you have a *store of consciousness* in your unconscious mind that contains both negative and positive seeds. Negative seeds are things such as fear, jealousy and anger. Positive seeds are things like joy, compassion and mindfulness. What grows into *mental formations* in your conscious mind depends on what gets watered.

We usually experience these *mental formations* as negative or positive emotions.

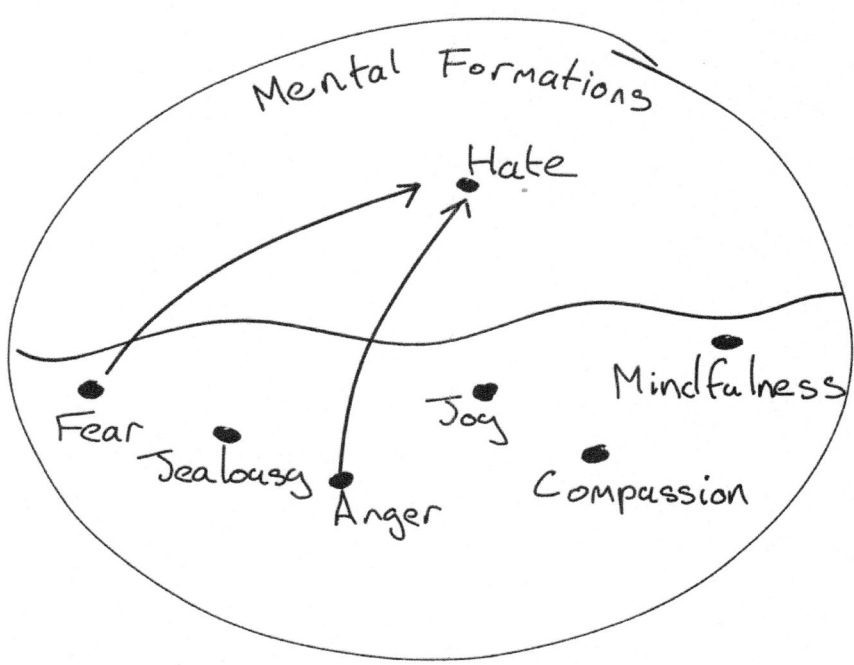

So, you can choose which seeds to water in your mind and those of others. Furthermore, the more frequently a particular seed is watered, the stronger it grows. This may last for a short time or it can become an ingrained habit.

Let's say you are commuting to work on public transport. On the way into work, you find your usual train has been cancelled because of a technical fault. You are about to step on an overcrowded carriage when someone barges past you, knocking you to one side. They have sprinkled a little drop of water on your seed of anger. You manage to squeeze on, but you are fuming all the way to work, sprinkling more water on the seed.

Later, at work, a senior colleague gives you feedback about a piece of work. You interpret their input as an attack on your competence rather than as an attempt to help you do better. They have poured a little more water on to your seed of anger. Throughout the day, you ruminate on what was said, pouring more water.

When the workday ends, the journey home is as challenging as it was on the way in. You arrive home and your loved one asks whether you bought the groceries needed for dinner. You react angrily, explaining what a terrible day you've had. Your loved one points out that it's not their fault. A blazing row ensues. The seed of anger has been watered throughout the day, growing more persistently each time.

How you deal with the seeds of anger can go beyond a bad day. Constant watering shapes the way we interact with the world. We all know someone we might describe as irritable. They are constant complainers and you have to be careful with your words when you talk to them.

Similarly, we all know people we think of as kind or caring – the sort of person you confide in easily, knowing they will not judge. They rarely give advice, but, somehow, after talking to them, things usually seem clearer.

These contrasting dispositions are not innate personality traits. They are the consequence of the regular watering of negative or positive seeds. And often we do a lot of that watering ourselves. How often have you blamed yourself for something that didn't work out as you intended?

So what can you do to be more content and help others be content? The first step is to be aware of the seeds you water in yourself and others. Be conscious of the words you say to others. Do they water positive or negative seeds?

Often you will find that you don't realise the impact of your words until afterwards. But when you do realise it, that moment of reflection and awareness makes you more likely to speak generously in future. Thich Nhat Hanh suggests you can ask yourself two questions before you speak:

- Will it help?
- Is it better than silence?

Find a way to water the positive seeds of others by saying something helpful or complimentary. If you don't genuinely feel either of those, try just keeping quiet.

It is more challenging to deal with the self-talk that waters your seeds because often you are unaware you are doing it. What you become aware of is the manifestation of that watering: the 'mental formations' of sentiments such as anger, resentment, maliciousness and jealously.

In Buddhism, which is fond of numbered lists, there are 51 positive and negative mental formations. For the curious, I've included the full list of these in Appendix C.

There are two things you can do: first, have a way of dealing with negative emotions when they arise; and, second, find ways to avoid watering them. Let's start by dealing with the first thing, because it's impossible to avoid negative emotions altogether.

Thich Nhat Hanh recommends that you cradle your negative emotions like a baby. 'Hello, anger, I know that you are there.' Then embrace the negative feeling with the energy of mindfulness. This can be done by being aware of your breathing. Bring yourself back to the present moment, not ruminating on a past that has gone or a future that hasn't arrived yet.

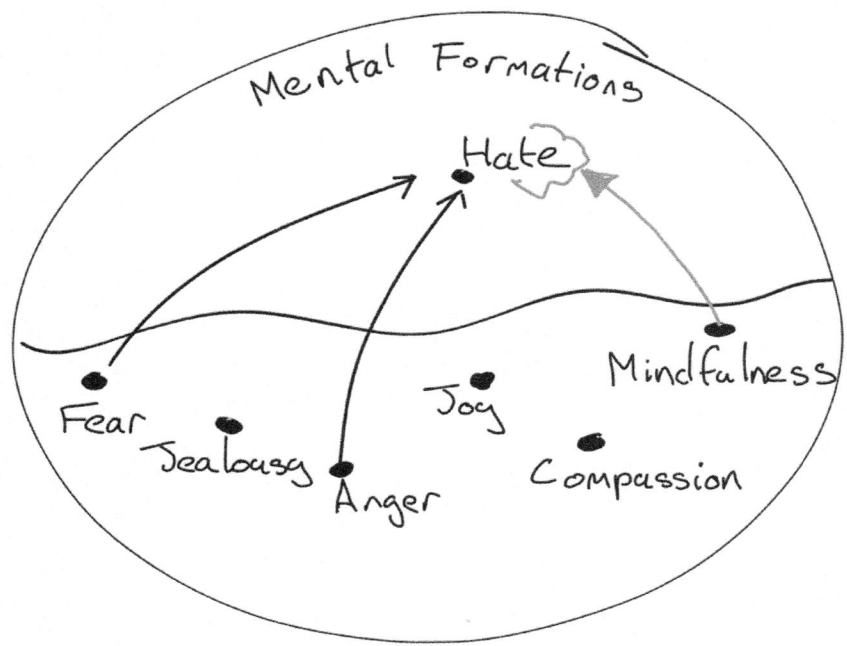

Mindful walking is an excellent way of doing this. Slow down your breathing and take one step on your in-breath and the next on your out-breath. As little as five slow steps will change your mental state. There is sound neuroscience behind this idea. Slowing down your physical behaviour delays your primitive fight-or-flight response. By the time you finish your breathing and walking, your brain realises there isn't an existential threat after all.

The critical thing required in order for this strategy to work is to accept that the negative emotion is present rather than to try and fight it. Telling yourself not to be angry to calm down only waters the seed of frustration at your inability to deal with whatever has occurred.

You don't have to be a Buddhist to do this. When I was a child and got angry, my mum used to tell me to count to 10. It's pretty much the same thing.

The second thing you can do is to water positive seeds and avoid watering negative ones. Contrary to what some people believe, we are not a selfish species. We have prospered on this planet because of our ability to collaborate. That's why it feels good to help someone else or to pay them a compliment. You can water your positive seeds by seeing others, and yourself, through the eyes of compassion.

You can stop watering your negative seeds by avoiding activities, situations, groups and individuals that you know will water them. For example, I know quite a few people who have stopped using Twitter because it is a constant flow of water for their negative seeds. More fundamentally, if you are unhappy at work, there comes a point when you have to ask yourself whether you can thrive or whether the garden's owner sees you as a weed.

If someone regularly waters your negative seeds and avoidance isn't feasible or desirable, another option is a heart-to-heart conversation. For most of us, this takes courage. However, the alternative is for those negative seeds, particularly resentment, to grow stronger.

If a negative emotion is still festering, despite trying mindful breathing and walking, explain to the other person the impact their actions and words are having on you. Ask them for their help to avoid this happening in the future. This simple request packs a big punch:

- It brings the unsaid to the surface.
- It identifies the impact on you.
- It identifies a cause, but doesn't do so in a way that apportions

149

blame.

- It focuses on what can be done in the future rather than dwelling on what happened.

- It engages the other person's innate desire to help others.

According to Thich Nhat Hanh, the root cause of a negative emotion is usually a *wrong perception* in you, the other person or both – or in other words, untested assumptions about what each of your believes.

Asking someone to water your positive seeds doesn't have to wait for a crisis. In some cultures, such as the UK, we might feel embarrassed to say something such as 'I like it when you…' or 'I feel energised/motivated when you…' But overcome your shyness and try it out. Don't make others, especially loved ones, guess what makes you tick. You'll be surprised by the results.

On one wedding anniversary, I brought home flowers. My wife said to me: 'I love it when you bring me flowers.' As it happened, on my way home from work on Fridays, I habitually walked straight past a flower seller. So the next Friday, I arrived home with flowers, for no particular reason other than I wanted to show love.

Walking home, I worried that she would say something like 'you only did it because I told you to'. Instead, she was delighted. After that, I brought home flowers every single Friday and she was always delighted that I did. I later found out she proudly told all of her friends that I regularly brought her flowers. Mind-reading is a tricky business, so let your loved ones know what waters your positive seeds.

At work, you can do something similar, using phrases like: 'I find it helpful when you…' The best time to do this is when a positive example happens. If you forget, don't let that deter you from saying it later. But focus on what you observed rather than your interpretation of it. For example, don't say 'you seemed annoyed when I talked about X'. It's better to say 'when I started to talk about X, you interrupted me with what seemed to be a raised voice'.

There is one last compelling way to avoid watering your negative seeds: change the way you interpret what feels like criticism. Treat it as feedback about something you did, not who you are. The former is an opportunity for improvement, whereas the latter is hurtful.

It's helpful to think about it in the other direction– when you want to help someone else, but they hear it as criticism of them as an individual. As Marshall Goldsmith says, 'it's not what you say, it's what they hear'.

Water the positive seeds in others and they will
water yours.

Key Points

- Water relationships regularly with your attention and presence.
- Successful change depends on good relationships.
- There is no substitute for face-to-face contact for your most important relationships.
- Beware of 'out of sight, out of mind'.
- Water the good seeds, not the bad seeds, in yourself and others.
- See feedback you get as coaching, not criticism.

Time-out

I want to interrupt the flow of the book at this point to remind you of something vital that I wrote when I started to describe the elements of gardening. As emotion plays such a central role in my examples, I also want to share the latest neuroscience on that topic.

Think Like a Gardener

First, here is the reminder. The purpose of the examples in Part Two, *The Elements of Gardening*, is to stimulate you to think like a gardener, not to tell you how to be a gardener. I have shared ideas and approaches that I hope you find useful and can perhaps apply to your change. But that would be a bonus.

The worst outcome for me would be if you go away from reading this book believing that it is complicated to think like a gardener, that you have to try to remember the ideas I have included. Thinking 'I need to this thing and then I need to that thing', as if it were a recipe for success. No matter how strongly I might appear to be advocating a particular idea or approach, I am merely sharing my enthusiasm for ideas and things that have worked for me in the past, in one or more situations.

The best possible outcome is that you remember the three characteristics of an ecosystem and that you use the elements of gardening as prompts for your ideas. So if your idea of, say, pruning is different from mine, that's terrific.

To save you flicking back, the three ecosystem characteristics are:

- Unpredictability
- Interdependence
- Limits of control

And the elements of gardening are:

- Plan
- Prepare the Soil
- Plant
- Prune
- Weed
- Water
- Stake
- Ensure Good Health
- Enjoy Your Harvest

Emotions

The second reason for interrupting the flow of the book is to share the very latest thinking on emotions, as they play such a central role in this book.

Lisa Feldman Barratt is a psychologist and neuroscientist who has spent much of her career studying emotions. As I write, she is a distinguished professor at Northeastern University in Boston in the US. In her 2017 book *How Emotions are Made*[42], she argues that emotions are concepts that we learn, rather than something with which we are born.

Emotions are our interpretation of two innate feelings of arousal and pleasure that are common to most animals. Thus, you learn that what you feel is happiness or anger in the same way as you learn that grass is green or the sky is blue. But rather than naming an attribute of grass, you put a name to a physical sensation in a particular situation. Below are some examples.

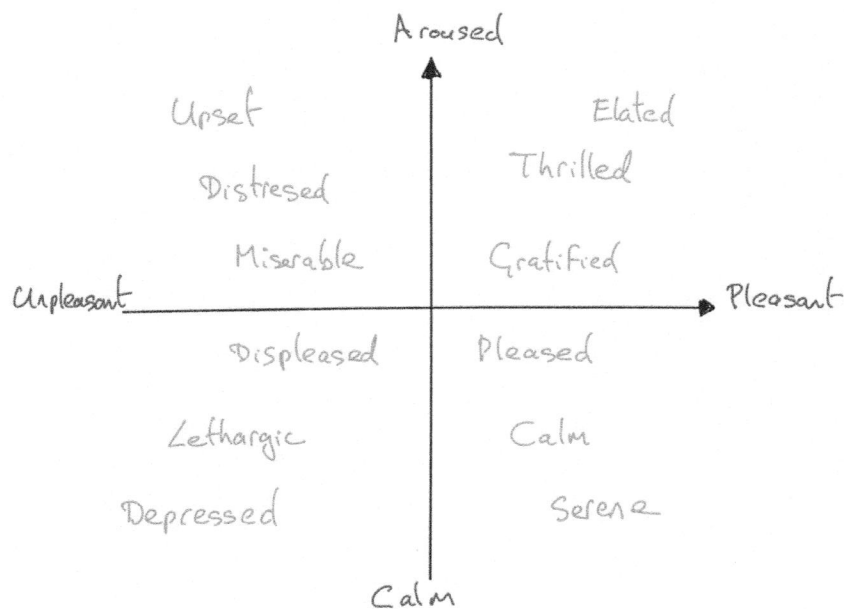

The reason this is important is that it means we have a degree of control over the emotions we feel. If we only have a name for green, then everything green is put into the same category, with the same associations. However, if we have different names for different types of green, such as emerald, sage and lime, we can understand and communicate at a more granular level.

So, for example, if we only have one word for anger, that's what we feel, with all of its associations. However, if we can subdivide anger it into less intense categories, such as frustration, irritation and exasperation, this may create an emotion with which it is easier to cope.

This view of emotions isn't arguing that feelings aren't real. What you have learned is as real as anything else you were born with or learned. It's merely that these emotions are neither fixed nor universal across culture.

Stake

What is Staking?

When I came to this element of gardening in Christopher Lloyd's list, I immediately saw a trellis and support canes in the ground. I thought: 'I'll call that chapter "Support" instead of "Staking", because it's more obvious.' But then I read Christopher's summary of *Staking*:

- What support will your plants need?
- When will they need that support?
- How will you guide your plant to grow in the direction and shape you desire?
- How will you restrict your plant within the available space?

The first two items are indeed about support, but the last two made me think about *constraints*. So, the first section in this chapter is about support, and I hope to highlight two less obvious ways of thinking about support. The second section is about constraints, real and imagined, imposed and self-imposed.

Support

Exercise

Let's start with the more obvious aspects of support. Think about your change.

Write down as many different types of support you think you need to achieve the outcome you want. Include support that you will need, as well as the support that others will need.

Then annotate each item on your list with a rough date for which you think that support will be needed and for how long it will be needed.

How did you get on? Below is a checklist to help you. Go through and update your list, if needed:

- People to help make it happen.
- Physical resources such as buildings, transport, materials, etc.
- Psychological support.
- Moral support.
- Critical friends.
- Expertise.
- Skills.
- Experience.
- Training.
- Coaching.

- Mentoring.

Stages of Change

The first, less obvious aspect of support is the transition stage of change. We can visualise where you are now and where we want to get to, but don't think deeply enough about managing the period in between. It's during that period of uncertainty that support is often most needed.

Evolution has programmed us to see uncertainty as a threat. Individuals and groups respond in two ways. First, defensively: freeze, fight or flight. Second, we try to resolve the uncertainty, often by clinging tightly to the status quo. Both responses can be obstacles to change.

In one of the programmes that I ran in retail banking, the change affected 30,000 people and for many of them, the transition state lasted as long as two years. This transition period was a massive opportunity to alienate people we needed to operate the vision. Consequently, we spent as much thought and energy on planning and managing the transition as we did on creating the vision.

When thinking about the support you and others need during the transition, a useful analogy comes courtesy of Swiss psychiatrist Elizabeth Kubler-Ross and her work with terminally ill patients. In her book *On Death and Dying*[43], she describes five stages experienced from the point of receiving a terminal diagnosis:

- Denial – It's not happening.
- Anger – Who's to blame? Why me?
- Bargaining – Give me another year and I'll reconcile with my sister.
- Depression – I am too sad to do anything.

- Acceptance – I'm at peace with what is coming.

Kubler-Ross has been at pains to point out that she never intended to imply that the stages are sequential or that all of the stages are experienced by everyone. However, if you search for her name, you'll see a diagram like the one below that does imply sequence:

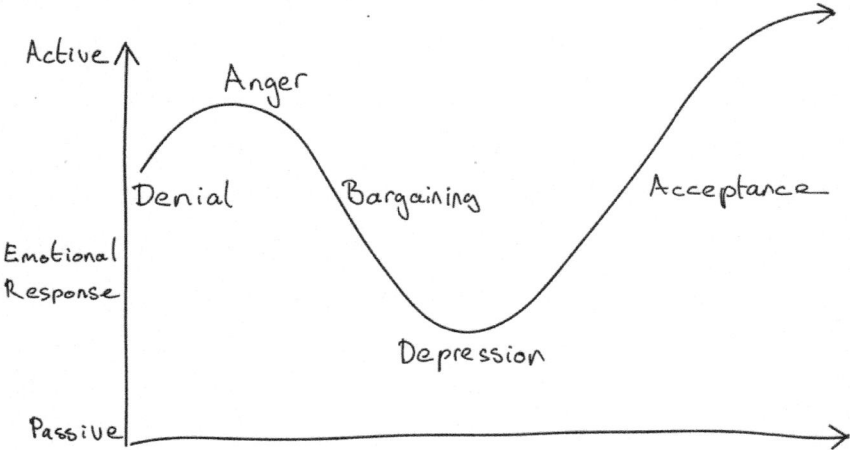

However, in management literature, you are likely to read that when you are faced with major change, you will progress sequentially through these emotional states. The speed of progression from one stage to the next, goes the narrative, will vary. And, according to this management version, you can find yourself stuck in one of the states or oscillating between them. This is what I was taught at business school.

And although you'll usually see the curve attributed to Kubler-Ross, it did not appear in *On Death and Dying* or the subsequent book *On Grief and Grieving*[44]. I've been unable to track down where it originated.

This curve has also been widely adapted in change management literature. The most common version is shown below. As with the other diagram, I've been unable to determine who first drew it, despite digging out the papers where it is supposed to have first appeared.

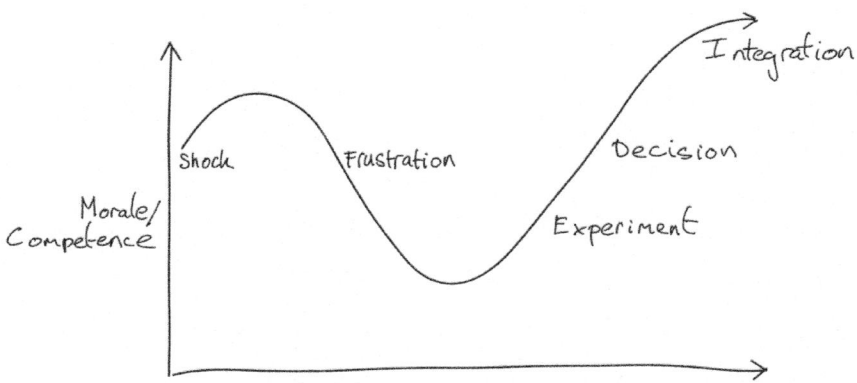

However, these misconceptions don't negate the usefulness of using Kubler-Ross' five stages to think about how you and others are affected by change. I just don't want you to fall into the ubiquitous trap of thinking the stages are a linear, interdependent progression. Dare I say it, the stages are more like an ecosystem than a machine!

So, returning to the theme of this chapter, Kubler-Ross' five stages can help to stimulate your thinking about what support you and others might need, but thinking like a gardener, not a production line.

In doing so, I think that the original five stages are much more useful than the management-speak adaptation. The original five stages put emotion centre stage and ask questions such as: who can I talk to and who will listen without judging? Who will be honest with me when I ask for feedback?

Death, dying and grief are powerful analogies you can use to explore these types of questions and invent lots of your own.

Exercise

Think about what the five stages might mean for your change.

Asking for Support

Recently, a client asked a colleague and me to create a change management course. The purpose of the course was to help their team of management consultants to manage change at a personal level. Thus, it focused on relationships rather than strategic change.

In a workshop to shape the content, one of the sponsors said it would be helpful to be able to show consultants how to ask for support when they get stuck. Everyone in the workshop agreed, but we had no ready-made idea in our back pocket. We said we'd look into it.

The next week, I started to look for an answer in management and psychology journals, but couldn't find a solution that fitted the bill. I found an understanding of the problem, but no solution.

The problem is that we tend to see a request for help as a failure. We see it as a failure of experience, skill or, worst of all, intellect. We think that a request for support signals that we are not up to it (this is a topic I will return to in the next chapter when I talk about a fixed mindset).

Now, if you are a super-confident person, you may not recognise this problem. Your belief in your ability is such that you readily ask for support because it doesn't dent your self-esteem. Everyone knows you're great, so if you ask for help, it must be necessary. If that's you, spare a thought for those mortals who worry about looking incompetent.

And if you are one of those mortals, don't go thinking that those super-confident individuals are quite what they seem. People, particularly at senior levels of an organisation, often suffer from *imposter syndrome*, a feeling that they are where they are as a result of a mistake that will come to light at any moment.

When I went to business school, I was fortunate to be in a closed full-time group of just over 20 people. It was an incredible learning opportunity. We spent the first week working with each other, debating case studies, and preparing and delivering presentations. At the end of the first week, I went home in a state of shock. I said to my wife: 'I am completely out of my depth.'

I went back the next week, an anxious wreck. On Thursday evening, having prepared our Friday presentations, we gathered in the bar and consumed enough alcohol to lower our inhibitions. It turned out that everyone felt the same. Each of us saw everyone else as brilliant and ourselves as a mistake.

But one person was missing. Not only was he the most senior of us, but he was also, by consensus, the brightest student and the best presenter by a very long way. The next day, he and I were driving home together. He asked what we'd discussed in the bar, such that we all looked so happy on Friday morning. With some embarrassment, I explained.

He told me that, for his whole career, he felt as if he were 'skating quickly over thin ice', expecting to fall through any second. He was relieved to find out he was not regarded as the dunce of the class by the rest of us.

So whether you are confident or not, there comes a time when you need to ask for support or you want to convince others that it's safe to ask for help. How can you do this?

The idea came to me out of nowhere and I hope you may find it useful. It's the use of a tool designed for decision-making, used in a different context. It known by the acronym FORDEC, which is used by passenger travel flight crew[45]. Lufthansa developed the approach after one of its in-flight aircraft nearly met with disaster. Here is an explanation of the acronym:

- **F**acts: What have you observed and what is the problem?
- **O**ptions: How could the problem be resolved?
- **R**isks: What are the pros and cons of each option?
- **D**ecide: Select a course of action.
- **E**xecute: Take action.
- **C**heck: Did the action resolve the problem?

The idea is that before asking for support, you think through the first three stages: Facts, Options and Risk.

Then, at the Decide stage, you present your thinking to the person from whom you are seeking help, ideally with a recommendation for action. If you are asking for help because you are unable to decide, you can simply say which way you are leaning based on what you have presented.

At that point, you jointly decide on the course of action and talk about how you will Check whether it worked after you Execute it.

I shared this idea with some of the people I coach with good results, both for themselves and those who work for them.

Often, when the person seeking support gets to the Decide stage, they conclude that they don't need help after all. Going through the structured thinking process dampens the freeze, fight-or-flight response that led to the original need for help.

When support was requested, the discussion that followed was usually more like a coaching conversation than a directive one. Sometimes, the visible thought process identified a learning need on the part of the requester.

I can't pretend I have carried out a scientific study of how well this works. But, anecdotally, it seems to significantly reduce the fear of being seen as unable to cope. Part of this is demonstrating that it's not an unthinking cry for help and another part is that it puts the task that's causing the problem, not the individual, under the microscope.

Before you ask for help, think FORDEC.

Accepting Support

The other side of the supported coin is how you deal with it when it is unsolicited.

One time, I had to give a presentation to the Board. It was my first ever Board presentation and I was nervous. In those days, we used to create a printed *deck* of slides to talk through at meetings. I prepared well in advance and had what I thought was a great storyline.

A few hours before the meeting, my boss wandered by and started flipping through the slides. He drew my attention to a couple of slides that he thought could be changed to strengthen the story.

I thought I had done an excellent job and was discouraged by what I heard as criticism. On top of that, I have always disliked doing things at the last minute because it gives no time to correct mistakes. If I followed my boss' advice, I'd have to rework the slides and print them all off again.

Consequently, my reaction was defensive. I said I thought the *deck* was fine. If what he had highlighted came up, I could talk about it. He tilted his head down slightly and looked at me over the top of his glasses. I knew that look and went off to change the slides like a child told to tidy his room.

When I presented those changed slides, they were the catalyst for vigorous debate amongst Board members. And often, because of the revised structure of the presentation, I was able to interrupt the debate to say that information contained in the following slides might help resolve the debate.

I looked across at my boss to get the 'I told you so' look. Instead, he had the look of a proud parent whose son had just scored a goal. I learned three things:

- My boss was coaching me to be better, not criticising me for being wrong.
- His feedback was about the task, not his perception of my overall capability or potential.
- He wanted to feel useful and make a contribution.

This completely changed the way I interpreted what he said to me in future. He was coaching, not criticising, and I began to seek out his input when faced with something tricky.

Many years later, my wife and I were with a group trekking in Nepal. I was the oldest in our group, but, I'd claim, one of the fittest. On one occasion, as we descended a steep path composed of giant stone steps, our guide held out his hand to help me balance, as he did for everyone, regardless of their age.

At first, I declined, as I wanted to be self-sufficient and didn't feel I needed help. Then I realised I was missing the point. I thought about how I felt those times I had offered someone support, only to have it rejected. I held out my hand and he smiled broadly, pleased to be able to help, thinking no less of me for accepting, just like my boss in the story above.

Whether you think you need help or not, sometimes it's best to accept it gracefully for the benefit of the person offering. And who knows, maybe you will find it helps you do something better!

Constraints

Constraints typically come in one of three guises:

- A genuine resource constraint within which you have to work.
- An imagined constraint in order to spark creativity.
- A self-imposed constraint.

Genuine Resource Constraints

After the Second World War, Japan's *Ministry of International Trade and Industry* (MITI) identified manufacturing as the critical driver needed to rebuild the economy and restore morale. Different groups of companies, known as *keiretsu*, were made responsible for various business sectors. One of these was Toyota.

Toyota was ear-marked for vehicle manufacture, but didn't have the resources to compete with the US giants such as Ford and General Motors. Out of necessity, Toyota had to find a way to reduce the cost of production. This constraint resulted in two world-changing manufacturing innovations.

First, in those days, a car production plant would have lots of cages, full to the brim with parts, waiting to be used on the assembly line. Toyota realised that every part sitting in a pile was money that was tied up. Each cage of parts was effectively a pile of cash doing nothing. So, the company set about finding ways of reducing the size of these piles and invented what popularly became known as *Just in Time* manufacturing.

Second, Toyota realised that a defective part, which could not be used, effectively meant paying for the same part twice: first to produce the defective part and then again to produce an acceptable part. With the help of two US engineers, W. Edwards Demming and Joseph Juran, who had been largely ignored in their own country, Toyota set about eliminating defective parts, or waste, through continuous improvement (using something called *statistical process control*).

The Toyota Production System was born. The US and European giants watched in disbelief as their customers forsook national loyalty for lower prices and better quality.

Had Toyota not faced a resource constraint, it is likely that it would have copied US methods of production and would never have created 'The Machine That Changed the World'.

Artificial Constraints

In their book *A Beautiful Constraint*[46], Adam Morgan and Mark Barden say that their 'aim is to show how constraints can be fertile, enabling and desirable. Why they are catalytic forces that stimulate exciting new approaches and possibilities.

Sometimes these constraints are real, as in the previous section. Or they may be self-imposed, as in the next section. But artificial constraints are also widely used by designers as a tool to take thinking outside the box. They ask the question: 'How could we do this if...?'

Imagine if General Motors had asked its engineers how they could reduce the cost of production prior to Toyota's invention of *Lean Production*. They would likely have identified incremental improvements, not something radically innovative.

However, imagine they are in a start-up venture. And for the enterprise to succeed, the cost per car has to be half that of a standard GM saloon. They will have to find radical, innovative solutions.

Every change initiative gets to the point where you have to come up with possible solutions. The problem is that these tend to be slightly different versions of the same thing rather than genuinely different options.

Large organisations often mandate that business cases for projects contain three different options. But what you usually get is the version the team wants, the gold-plated version and the sub-optimal version.

I like to use constraints to prompt divergent thinking and give different groups different questions, such as:

- How would you do if you were in a start-up?
- What would you do if you only had three months?
- What would you do if you only had a certain amount of money?
- How would you do it in order to be fully recyclable?
- How would you do it so that the price would be below a certain limit?

It's rare that any one question yields the desired answer. The best solution usually results from combing elements of each answer.

Exercise

How do you go about your change if:

- You have no money to spend?
- You only have half the time or money you think you need?
- You use your idea to start a new business?
- You have to deliver something that is ready to be used within four weeks?
- You can do everything you see on *Star Trek*?

Design Constraints

A design constraint is a choice you make voluntarily. Think back to the iPhone in the chapter 'Plan'. Steve Jobs's brief to the development team was that the new device had to be a phone and that it had to fit in a pocket.

There were many more constraints in the vision for the iPhone's ancestor, the *Sony Walkman*. Introduced in 1979, it revolutionised the way we consume music.

In 1978, Sony was already a successful global business. Consequently, its 70-year-old co-founder and Honorary Chairman, Masaru Ibuka, was a frequent air traveller. He was also a music lover and never flew without Sony's *TC-D5* stereo audio cassette recorder. However, it weighed 1.7 kg (or 3.75 lb), so Ibuka wanted something smaller and lighter[47].

Ibuka asked Sony's Deputy President, Norio Ohga, to create a simple, playback-only, stereo version of *The Pressman*, the small, mono tape recorder that Sony launched in 1978.

Ibuka tested the resulting prototype on his next trip to the US. Delighted with his experience, he showed it to Sony Chairman and co-founder Akio Morita. 'Try this', he said, 'Don't you think a stereo cassette player that you can listen to while walking around is a good idea?'

Morita did indeed think it was a good idea and in February 1979 he called a meeting at Sony Headquarters. Invited to the meeting were a group of predominantly young engineers. In Japan's hierarchical business culture, they were more than a little apprehensive to know why the Chairman has summoned them.

Morita held up a modified Pressman:

> *'This is the product that will satisfy those young*
> *people who want to listen to music all day. They'll*
> *take it everywhere with them, and they won't care*
> *about recording functions. If we put a playback-only*
> *headphone stereo like this on the market, it'll be a*
> *hit. Our target market is students and other young*
> *people. We must launch it before the summer*
> *vacation at a price similar to the Pressman, which*
> *means less than 40,000 yen [40,000 yen was nearly*
> *£300. The TC-D5 was 100,000 yen or £750].'*

That was Morita's vision for the Walkman. How many design constraints can you count? I made it six, dictated by Morita's interpretation of what would sell. But within those explicit constraints, the engineers had the freedom to create whatever fulfilled the vision.

The vision for your change will always have some constraints. But the higher the number of limitations, the fewer the solutions that will fulfil that vision. That's fine as long as those constraints are real and not untested assumptions. The Walkman's restrictions were so explicit that they were described on Sony's company history webpage.

However, implicit constraints often inhibit creativity. These constraints result from untested assumptions made as you journey from why to how.

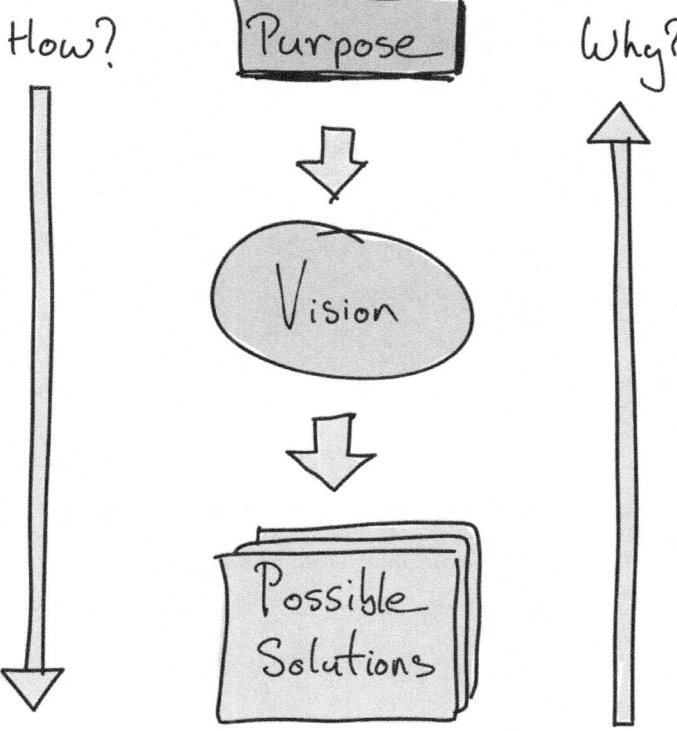

Before the iPhone, every mobile phone had a keyboard, mostly numbers with letters above that could be used to write text messages. The exception was the *BlackBerry* and its tiny keyboard; so addicted were business emailers to this device that it became nicknamed the 'Crackberry'.

So it would have seemed natural for the iPhone development team to assume that their new device would need a physical keyboard. Perhaps the team leader creates a keyboard development team. The group worries whether the keys are too small; would they be better on a fold-out, clamshell section? Do the keys have the right amount of resistance to touch? Should they abandon the QWERTY layout?

Someone armed with the five whys asks: 'Why do we need a physical keyboard? What is the purpose our team is aiming to fulfil?'

In my experience, constraints often occur early on in a project, based on untested assumptions. Then further down the timeline, everyone has forgotten that the premise wasn't tested. The constraint has become part of the fabric and goes unchallenged. Or sometimes the business or technology environment has changed, such that a critical assumption is no longer valid.

The solution, I believe, is to heed the following advice:

Make major assumptions and constraints explicit.
If you are working in a team, put the big ones on
the wall and revisit them regularly.

Key Points

- Ask what support is needed at the different stages of change.
- Use FORDEC to ask for support.
- Learn to accept support when offered.
- Use constraints to stimulate creativity.
- Watch out for assumptions that create implicit constraints.
- Make key constraints explicit and review regularly.

Ensure Good Health

Introduction

In a garden, there are two more things you need to do to ensure that you maintain healthy growth before you can move on and enjoy your harvest:

- Nourish the plants.
- Combat diseases and pests.

The two are linked, as an undernourished plant is more susceptible to pests and diseases than a healthy plant. Similarly, a plant attacked by pests or diseases may need additional nutrients in order to help it fight back.

To illustrate nourishment, I'll return to the Tokyo project I talked about in the chapter 'Water', and use trust as an example of an essential nutrient for growth.

After that, I'll interpret disease as being something that isn't visible to the naked eye, but whose effects are all too apparent. I'll use two analogies to illustrate this: a group culture and a fixed mindset.

Finally, I'll interpret pests as visible inhibitors of growth. This usually means individuals and groups, so I'll talk about the main reason that people typically oppose change – and that's fear.

This chapter is a little longer than the others but it's commensurate with the energy that needs to be devoted to this stage of gardening.

Nourishment

As you may recall, I made monthly visits to Tokyo to 'water' the relationship. And although those visits reduced the frequency of significant issues, interpersonal relationships were still stiff and formal. Now and again, a seemingly major problem would arise out of the blue and would have to be unpicked. The connection needed something more than just the water of attention.

The missing nutrient was trust. Our Managing Director told me that in Japanese corporate culture, a person speaks on behalf of the whole company, not just himself or herself. So the puzzle was how to build the personal trust I believed to be the foundation of success for all large change endeavours.

In a previous programme, I stumbled upon the idea of having off-the-record, fireside chats with key stakeholders, including clients and suppliers. With never more than two or three of us together, we put aside the party line and were honest about mutual organisational failings. Instead of defending respective performance, we focused on our shared goal of a successful project outcome.

The next time I was in Tokyo, I took a deep breath and asked the client Project Manager, through the translator, if we could have a weekly *informal meeting*. These, I said, would be off-the-record meetings in which we spoke personally rather than as a representative of our respective organisations.

To my relief, he agreed, with one condition. He wanted to keep a record of the agreements and actions from the meeting to ensure that nothing got lost. That record, he said, would be just between the translator and us. If he wanted to share something with his organisation, he told me, he would seek my agreement in advance.

Despite his reassurance, I was nervous the first time I owned up to a mistake by our team. The problem we caused gave our client much grief and resulted in much executive-level hot air flowing from Tokyo to London.

He reciprocated by telling me that the impact of our mistake had been exaggerated. It had been escalated by an executive in Tokyo who wanted to demonstrate to his boss and peers in Tokyo that he was a 'serious and concerned individual'. His candour surprised me. He knew his career would be over if I repeated what he had said to anyone else.

That was on my third trip to Tokyo. After that, we had an informal meeting every week, three times a month by telephone and at least once a month face to face in Tokyo. Now and then, he would say: 'Gary-san, I would like to share what you said. Are you happy with that?' Most of the time, the answer was yes. At other times, it was 'not just yet; let me talk to some people first'.

I also set up a weekly informal meeting with the Project Manager of our Japanese delivery partner. The nurturing of that particular relationship paid dividends at a critical point in the project. Our partner encountered a significant technical issue that threatened the client's target launch for the new derivatives exchange.

Our partner's technicians thought the problem was our software, and our technicians thought it was theirs. But before it got to the public finger-pointing stage, we went to a noodle bar and hatched a plan. I would fly

177

our best network specialists to Tokyo to work with our partner's top people.

After four days of difficult detective work, the problem was found to be a software error in a ubiquitous piece of networking hardware called a *router*. The hardware supplier had caused the problem. The two teams, from our partner and ourselves, embarked on a celebratory tour of Tokyo's many bars and formed relationships that were to serve the project well.

In a real garden, a plant will sometimes do quite well with just water, because the soil is already fertile with nutrients – for example, if you are growing your plant in a pot filled with fresh compost.

If, however, you plant in ground where plants have been grown before, the previous season's plants will have used up many the nutrients. So, if you want your flowers and vegetables to thrive, they will benefit from additional nutrients as well.

This is much like some situations at work, where short-term cost-cutting has failed to replace the resources necessary for long-term growth. Or perhaps a change initiated is driven through, but uses up all of the goodwill needed to sustain it in the long term.

Note that although I wrote about the need for watering and nourishment separately, they are often combined, as they were in my relationships in Japan. Similarly, preparing the soil and planting are not separate activities from nourishment. When you prepare the soil, it's common to dig in some compost to provide nourishment and to aerate the soil in order to welcome the roots you have teased out.

I have written about each element of gardening separately, but in a healthy garden, they take place simultaneously, supporting each other, as you adapt to a changing environment.

What grows depends on our skill as a gardener. As Thich Nhat Hanh points out:

Never blame a plant for not growing. You have to provide right conditions and that applies just as much to people and teams as it does to plants.

Exercise

- What sort of nutrients will your change need as it grows?
- How often are they needed?
- How will you ensure they are delivered?

Culture

Culture is a word that comes up a lot in the context of organisational change. You'll hear people say things such as:

- 'The culture is resistant to change.'
- 'The culture doesn't encourage innovation.'
- 'It's a conservative culture.'
- 'We need to change the culture.'

We understand what is meant by those types of phrases because we see that culture reflected daily in the behaviours of those around us at work. But how can you go about changing a group's culture? Is it even possible to change a group's culture? When I was at business school, I got an opportunity to answer those questions.

The story actually starts about three months before I went to business school. I was given an interim assignment to work on a *culture change programme* aimed at my banking employer's 3,000-strong IT department. It's one of the least rewarding jobs I have ever done.

In the 1990s, culture change programmes were all the rage. Our bank had hired management consultants to help change the culture into something 'more dynamic and more commercial'. At least I think that's what it was about, although I was never totally sure.

To achieve this, the *top team* spent a couple of days at the seaside and came up with a mission statement and a list of values to be 'cascaded' to the whole department. I can vividly recall that one of the values was *being more commercial*. In a moment, you'll understand why I remember. The other values were similarly nebulous, such as *collaboration*.

The consultants then designed a series of workshops to explain the mission and values to every single one of the 3,000 people and to exhort staff to *live the values*. One of my roles was to support the workshops, although fortunately not to run them.

One day, I went to a workshop in a department then known as *computer operations*. It was the mid-1990s, when mainframes dominated. The most common form of data storage was magnetic tapes and there was someone in the workshop whose primary job was to load and unload tapes.

'How can I be more commercial?', he asked. 'What would I actually do differently?' He had asked the killer question for anyone wanting to change culture: what is it exactly you want me to do differently?

I realised then that the bank's culture change programme was doomed to failure. But it left me with a conundrum that would bug me for another six months: just what is culture and can one change it?

When I got to business school, we had a module named *organisational behaviour*. One of my fellow students, from a global energy company, said his organisation had gone through a successful culture change programme that was a major success. Given my experience up to that point, I was sceptical but curious. I decided to use the module's assessment assignment to compare the culture change programme I had experienced at first hand with the one my fellow student referred to.

And because we were both sponsored to be at business school by our respective organisations, we were granted access to a lot of people, including executives, in both organisations. It turned out that people at all levels within the energy company regarded the programme as a success. There was a surprising lack of cynicism in this organisation that had gone from being state-owned to a world leader.

In parallel to the interviews in the energy organisation, I read as much academic literature about culture as I could find. Most of it talked about behaviours, symbols and artefacts. Then I came across a book entitled *Organizational Culture and Leadership* by MIT professor Ed Schein[48], which unlocked the secret.

The roots of culture, Schein wrote, are a set of assumptions and beliefs that get abstracted into values. What he means by this is that if, for example, a charity experiences its best results from humorous advertisements on *YouTube*, it will reasonably assume that it's a medium that works particularly well for it. That assumption might then become a value: *viral marketing works best*. And it's that value that gets communicated and becomes part of the culture, without having to repeat the whole story of cause and effect.

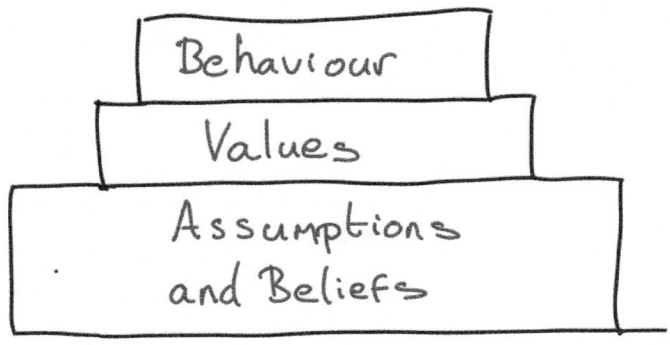

Schein went on to say that:

Group culture is collectively learned experience.

In other words, the roots of a group's culture are not an aggregation of personal values; it is assumptions and beliefs that result from shared experience.

The corollary is that you can change culture if you can engineer experiences that change assumptions and beliefs, or create new ones where none existed before. That's exactly happened at what the energy company.

The Director of the Oil and Gas Exploration Division had set a five-year challenge to reduce the cost of extracting a barrel of oil by a third. The size of the reduction meant that existing continuous improvement processes would not be sufficient to achieve the goal. The organisation would need to rethink the way it worked.

The Director created a central support team, drawn from a variety of different disciplines. The team had a strong bias towards process and systems visualisation, prototyping and experimentation rather than documentation.

However, the role of the support team wasn't to initiate change or do any of the work to change things. The support team was there to provide operational units with the tools to help them think differently. Someone who had been in the support team told me 'in the early days, we used to sit there waiting for someone to walk into our office. We played a lot of table tennis'.

But some early adopters did ask for help and after some successes, it wasn't long before the support team had to increase in size.

The Exploration Division achieved the five-year challenge in three years. The Director of the Division was soon the company's new CEO.

Interestingly, when I visited the Exploration Division, the walls were still covered in hand-drawn pictures on long lengths of paper. The images of processes and systems were still in use, even though the goal had been achieved some time before.

Seen through Ed Schein's lens, the Director had created a stretch target, together with an environment that encouraged collaboration and experimentation.

As part of my research, I ran a workshop with some of the operational units to find out how things had changed, without explicitly mentioning culture. But the topic of culture came up almost immediately. 'Before', said one of the participants, 'it was an individualistic culture, but now it's collaborative.' I asked whether they regarded collaboration as a core value and there was vigorous agreement from everyone.

The difference between this organisation and the bank was that the value had a specific meaning. It meant working across boundaries, offering to help others and not apportioning blame when things didn't work. There was no need to put it on a poster because the value was lived daily.

Changing culture is a job for a gardener. In the case of the energy company, even though the *mission* had been top-down, the soil had been prepared by putting in the support team. New assumptions and beliefs were roots that were teased out through experimentation, figuring out what would and wouldn't grow.

A footnote to the story about the energy company is that there was never a stated consequence of not achieving the mission. I have a sneaking feeling that the mission was created by someone very smart with the specific goal to change the culture.

Although I read Ed Schein's book in 1993, it was originally published in 1985. It is now in its fifth edition, illustrating how well his thinking has stood the test of time.

However, I read something recently by Dave Gray in his book *Liminal Thinking*[49] that I think enriches Schein's viewpoint:

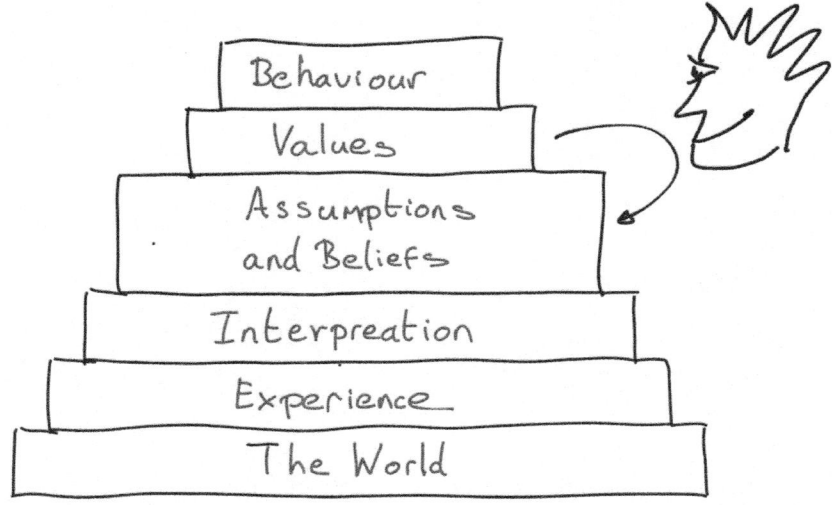

Gray points out that assumptions and beliefs are rooted in the soil of experience and our interpretation of that experience. And our interpretation is, in turn, seen through the lens of our existing assumptions and beliefs.

So, if you want to make a change, it's helpful to understand those existing assumptions and beliefs. And if they are deeply embedded, such as in national culture, you may need to work with them rather than try to change them.

Before my first business visit to Japan, I was lucky to receive some invaluable cultural awareness training, along with some of my colleagues. So when I asked my client if we could institute informal meetings, it was something new rather than an attempt to change the usual Japanese meeting culture.

A couple of years later, our company merged with similar companies from France and the Netherlands. The newly formed company instituted mandatory cultural awareness training, with workshops that included all three nationalities. The results were predictably hilarious and valuable.

If you are interested in the differences between national cultures, I recommend two books:

- *The Culture Map: Decoding How People Think, Lead, and Get Things Done across Cultures* by Erin Meyer[50].
- *Rule Makers, Rule Breakers: How Tight and Loose Cultures Wire Our World* by Michele Gelfand[51].

However, do take care not to fall into the trap of stereotyping. It's good to be aware of cultural norms, but keep in mind that everyone is an individual. Just think about how you differ from what might be the stereotypical norms in your own culture.

I want to add one last element to this discussion of culture and that's the power of stories. That's how culture often defines itself – through the stories that are told. The story I told earlier about the global energy company was repeated to me by multiple people within that organisation. It had become an organisational legend.

People and groups who oppose change do so because their cultural pyramid is different from yours. So avoid thinking of people or groups as pests and try to understand why they think what they think.

As the Dalai Lama once said: 'I already know what I think. If I listen I may find out something new.'

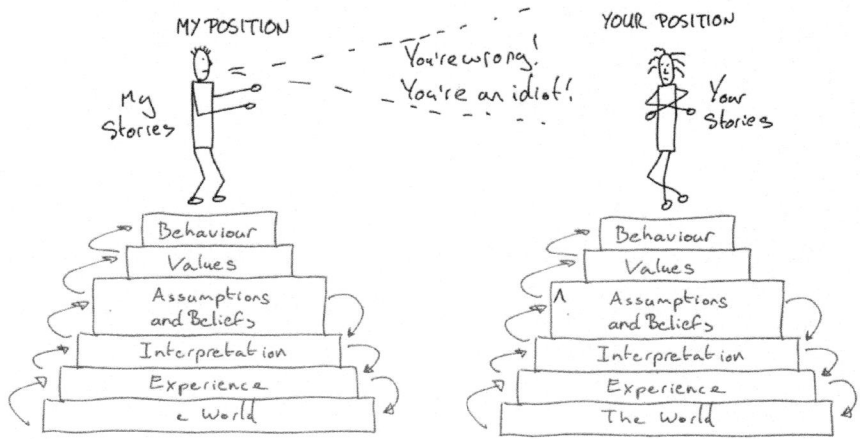

Exercise

Use the cultural pyramid above to think about the context for your change and in particular what assumptions and beliefs already exist.

Now think about how you can find out whether you are correct by talking to those involved and affected.

If you need to change these assumptions and beliefs, how could you create a shared experience that does so?

A Fixed Mindset

A fixed mindset[52] is an enemy of personal growth that can afflict you or members of your team. It's been my unseen enemy since my school days and I still battle with it today.

Unfortunately, however, the term *fixed mindset* and its counterpart, a *growth mindset*, seem to be losing their meaning as they become part of management-speak. In particular, a growth mindset is fast coming to simply mean an openness to new ideas and a desire to learn.

A friend of mine told me that 'growth mindset' was recently used as one of the evaluation criteria in his annual appraisal, scored between one and five. So, obviously, everyone wants a good score and scoring people low creates a lot of hassle and disputes. And in any case, a fixed mindset obviously sounds like a bad thing, so who is going to own up to that?

The problem is that many of us have a fixed mindset in at least one aspect of our lives without realising it. Let's run a quick test. Can you answer 'yes' to any of the following questions:

- Are you poor at mathematics?
- Do you not have a talent for art?
- Are you no good at sport?
- Are you not a creative type of person?
- Are you not good at languages?
- Do you have a poor sense of direction?
- Are you not a good cook?
- Do you have a bad memory?
- Do you have poor hand-to-eye coordination?
- Are you not good with maps?
- Are you useless with technology?

If you answered 'yes' to any of those questions, you probably have a fixed mindset in at least one aspect of your life. If you believe you have reached the limit of your innate capability in any of the skills referred to in the question, you definitely have a fixed mindset in that area.

Professor Carol Dweck has spent most of her 30-year career researching how children and young people learn. What she discovered is as applicable to adults as it is to children. She argues that our upbringing and education instils in us one of two mindsets. The picture below describes the characteristics of each mindset:

Fixed ←— INTELLIGENCE —→ Growth

Avoid failure ←—— CHALLENGES —→ Opportunity to learn

Give up easily ←— OBSTACLES —→ Persistence

Unecessary if
good enough ←—— EFFORT —→ Essential for mastery

Get defensive ←—— FEEDBACK —→ Opportunity to
learn and grow

Threat ←—— OTHERS —→ Inspiration

The essence of a fixed mindset is the belief that intelligence is innate rather than acquired. It's usual for us to get labelled as bright, average or slow based on a few tests early in life. After that general classification, we often get labelled as good, average or slow for particular topics, such as mathematics, languages and art. Those general and specific classifications become self-fulling prophecies.

That labelling, argues Dweck, usually starts with the language parents and teachers use when we are learning – for example, a parent or teacher who lavishes praise on a child who did well in a mathematics test, telling them how clever they are. What they should do, says Dweck, is to tell the child they did really well in the test and deserved it because they worked really hard; next time it'll be something harder to stretch them more. Make it about hard work and the task, says Dweck, not the child's identity.

This, of course, plays through into our adult self-talk. We extrapolate a few learning experiences into universal truths about our ability. If you have ever said out loud 'no-one gives me a harder time than me', you'll know exactly what I mean. Let me use myself as an example.

In the early stages of my education, I found mathematics easy. At the age of 11, teachers were already telling my parents: 'Gary is good at maths. He likes art, but he's not very good at art. He should stick to maths. That's where his strength lies.'

That was fine with me. I liked maths because I found it was easy and, in particular, it took me minimal effort to do the work. This is very handy if you are lazy like I am. I just turned up and breezed through. Test results had determined the course of my education by the time I was 12 years old.

By the time I was 17, I was still better at maths than most people. But my grades were no longer the straight As to which I had become accustomed. I began to wonder whether I had reached the limit of my capability. I was oblivious to the impact of doing homework while listening to Led Zeppelin at full blast or my discovery of alcohol and the opposite sex.

I was still good enough to study *civil engineering* at university. But the maths got harder and *fluid mechanics* caused me to raise the white flag. I decided I was now beyond my capability and flunked my second year.

When I returned for my third year, my confidence in mathematics was shot. I chose those electives modules that had the least mathematical content.

From the age of 11, I had gone through life labelling myself as good, bad or limited in almost everything I did. I was good at maths, up to a point. I was rubbish at foreign languages. I was good at basketball and rugby, but was no good at anything that involved a racket or a club. I was terrible at art. To this day, I battle against a fixed mindset. If you look at most of the characteristics of a fixed mindset in the picture above, you'll recognise most of them in my story.

Paradoxically, at school, I had a growth mindset when it came to rugby and basketball. We had a gifted teacher who created a growth environment. And although we were a comparatively small school, we usually had representatives in the national school teams of both sports, including myself in basketball.

I should add that I had incredibly supportive parents and teachers, to whom I will always be grateful. I somehow squeezed into the best state school in our area. I was the first of my generation, from my sort of background, to go to university. I didn't know a single person who had gone to university before I got on the train to travel 200 miles from London to Leeds.

I was lucky compared to the peers I grew up with, so I am not complaining. But I also know that I could have done a lot better if I had a growth mindset. This was confirmed for me when I did a master's degree some 15 years after my first degree and graduated with distinction.

By then, although I hadn't yet discovered Dweck's work, I had learned to separate the tasks I do from my identity. What I mean by that is that if

I do something well or poorly, I don't take it as a judgement on my overall ability.

When I first learned to play poker, I was successful straight off the bat. It was tempting to see myself as a natural, destined to rake in the cash. But there is much luck involved in poker and when I took it more seriously, my results nosedived. It turned out I wasn't a poker genius, nor was I an idiot – I was average at the level at which I played.

So, I worked hard on my game and gradually went up through the levels. Instead of beating myself up when I lost, I asked myself what I could learn from the way I played a specific hand. Note that in poker, you sometimes make the right decisions but get the wrong result, because luck is involved.

In a work situation, you might have a task to give a presentation. Let's say that afterwards, your boss tells you that the content was fine, but it was boring. If you have a fixed mindset, you might label yourself as a lousy presenter and avoid doing presentations in the future. I know plenty of talented people who are afraid of public speaking because of one or two bad experiences.

However, if you have a growth mindset, you'll recognise that this one presentation had not gone as you had hoped. And instead of telling yourself you are a terrible presenter, you'll see it as an opportunity to seek out feedback and advice in order to learn how to do a similar task better next time. And if you really have a growth mindset, you'll look for more opportunities to present, so that you can get better.

A growth mindset separates how well you do a specific task from a false definition of innate limitation.

Professor Dweck isn't saying that we can all be Mozart if we try hard enough. What she is saying is that many of us get nowhere near our full potential because of our self-limiting beliefs.

There is one prominent dissenter who dismisses the concept of a growth mindset as a 'gimmick'. Robert Plomin, Professor of Psychology at King's College London, argues that genes determine ability[53]. Forget nurture, argues Plomin, as it makes little difference[54].

It's not a view shared by most other academics, such as neuroscientist David Eagleman, who believe that although genes have an influence on performance, it is small compared to that of environmental factors.

At the start of his book, *Livewired: The Inside Story of the Ever-Changing Brain*[55], Eagleman sets out his view, "Our machinery isn't fully preprogramed, but instead shapes itself by interacting with the world. As we grow, we constantly rewrite our brain's circuitry to tackle challenges, leverage opportunities, and understand the social structures around us."

I side with Dweck and the other Eagleman, for two reasons: first, my own experience; and, second, *The Khan Academy*, the pre-eminent online school for mathematics (and now a host of other subjects).

The Khan Academy started by accident. In his spare time, Salman Khan was giving maths lessons to his nieces and nephews. To save him time, he found a way of recording his talk-and-chalk lessons as videos. To share them, he posted them on YouTube. Others saw them and liked them, so he structured them into what he jokingly named The Khan Academy.

Things took off big time when Bill Gates told a conference audience in Aspen that his children used The Khan Academy. Now it's a fantastic free online resource, across a range of subjects, supported by Microsoft, Google and public donations.

However, the point of this story is that The Khan Academy also now works together with schools, which integrate the platform into their curriculum. And because The Khan Academy is a digital platform, the school version enables teachers to monitor progress.

The data collected showed a surprising thing. Those who struggled with early lessons but persisted were often the best performers in the long run. They would watch the same video again and again until the penny dropped. Only then would they move on.

In contrast, those who found the initial lessons easy often floundered later on because they associated their performance with innate ability rather than the result of hard work and persistence. Whatever Robert Plomin believes, there is plenty of evidence that a fixed mindset prevents a great many of us from achieving our true potential, innate or otherwise!

Think of almost anything you can do well, from walking to riding a bike or playing a musical instrument, and you will find a path paved with trial and error. So, we have all had a growth mindset at one time or another. Yet when it comes to work, a fixed mindset is often a 'disease' lurking in our garden.

I'll leave the last work to Eagleman, "Each year, there are thousands of other children with [Albert Einstein's] potential but are exposed to cultures, economic conditions, or family structures that don't give sufficiently positive feedback. And we don't call them Einsteins".

Fear

People and groups usually oppose change out of fear, not bloody-mindedness. It might be a fear of losing something, such as employment, income, status, safety, power, health or a combination of all of these. Or it could be the fear of coping with new responsibilities, commitments, skills and people.

Often it's simply the intrinsic fear of change – any change. That's because fear is a Stone-Age, emotional response to an apparent threat, not a conscious choice. When we notice a difference in our environment, our subconscious mind decides, in an instant, whether it might be a threat. The default setting is that a change is a threat until proven otherwise.

Only when the perception of a threat has passed does the logical mind review what happened and add it to your mental database. Then the next time you encounter something similar, your subconscious consults that database before responding. But the default is still that a change is a threat, because 'probably not a threat' isn't a great survival strategy. We need 'definitely not a threat'.

So, if you are proposing a change and someone is opposed to it, there are a few things you can do. The most important is to acknowledge that the fear is real and valid. But telling someone that they have nothing to fear will only annoy them, because it implies they are being irrational, which they will hear as an insult.

And if you quickly follow up with a list of reasons why they have nothing to fear or why the change is an excellent opportunity for them, you'll push them into a corner. While in fear mode, they will be reacting subconsciously, inventing reasons to escape rather than calmly processing logic. To make matters worse, those subconsciously fabricated reasons for the opposition will become entrenched. That's because, as Professor Robert Cialdini points out in his seminal book *Influence*[56], we all have a strong drive to be consistent with what we have said or done before.

The best way to acknowledge fear is empathy. Show that you genuinely want to understand why they are opposed to the change.

And keep in mind that they may well have good reasons for feeling the way they do that you need to address. If that sounds a bit wishy-washy, let me tell you that empathy is a core technique used by modern-day terrorist and hostage negotiators.

Two British academics, Laurence and Emily Alison, were given access to over 1,000 hours of videotaped interrogations of terrorist suspects. Their findings reshaped interrogation technique across the world, although this came as no surprise to seasoned professionals.

After eight months of rigorous analysis, they found that the 'yield' of information from interrogation was strongly correlated to the degree of empathy. And that means showing you are genuinely interested in what the other person has to say, asking questions, listening to answers and asking follow-up questions. Going through the motions is transparent and doesn't work.

In one of the interrogations, a terrorist suspect with information that could save lives refused to cooperate. Below is an abridged version of the conversation, published in *The Guardian* newspaper in December 2018[57]. You can find the original online and I recommend doing so.

'Tell me why I should tell you', says the suspect. 'You don't know how corrupt your own government is – and if you don't care, then a curse upon you.'

'I am asking you these questions because I need to investigate what has happened and know what your role was in these events', says the interviewer.

'Why are you asking me these questions? Think carefully about your reasons', says the suspect.

This fruitless ping-pong continues until a different interviewer takes over. First he sets out the facts and then says: 'I don't know the details of what happened, why you may have felt it needed to happen, or what you wanted to achieve by doing this. I'd like you to help me understand. Would you tell me about what happened?'

'That is beautiful', says the suspect. 'Because you have treated me with consideration and respect, yes I will tell you now. But only to help you understand what is really happening in this country.'

The key in the lock was to express a genuine desire to understand the other person's point of view and listen without judging.

Chris Voss, the FBI's former chief hostage negotiator, endorses the central role of empathy. In his entertaining book on negotiation, *Never Split the Difference*[58], he recounts stories of negotiations with kidnappers in locations that range from New York to the Philippines and Ecuador.

The most important factor, says Voss, who now teaches negotiation at Harvard University, is to build a rapport with the kidnappers. You need to understand their needs and empathise with their point of view, he says. When you can reflect their point of view to them and hear them say 'that's right', you have the basis for negotiation.

The culture pyramid I presented at the start of the chapter is a useful model to help you explore someone else's point of view. Use open questions to tease out their assumptions and beliefs, and explore the experiences that shaped them.

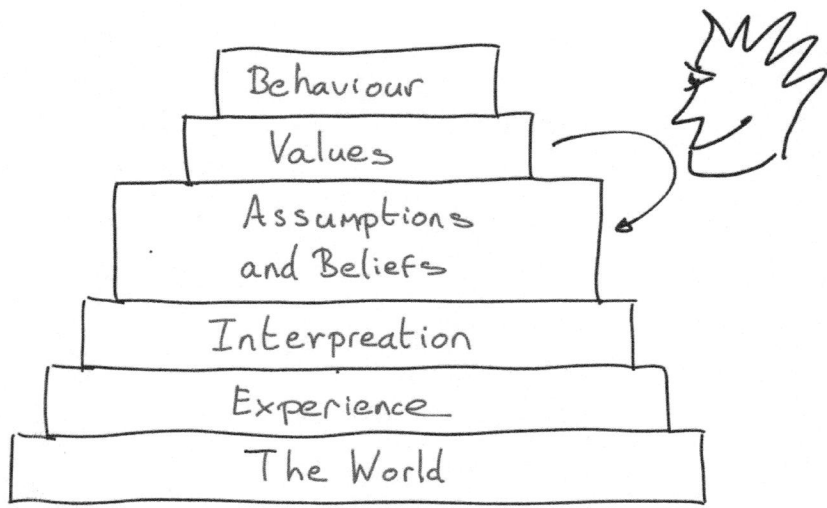

Terrorist and kidnapping negotiation might seem to be a long way away from a change at work. But when you encounter resistance from people, the goal is the same: you want them to open the door to a different viewpoint and behaviour. To achieve that, you first have to listen to and understand them, and show that you do.

It's worth keeping in mind that the prospect of losing something carries more emotional weight than gaining something of equal value. Say, for example, you could win or lose £1,000 on the flip of a coin. Would you take the bet? You have a 50% chance of gaining £1,000. Most people wouldn't take the bet because they want to avoid the loss. But how much would you need to win to make it worth the risk of losing £1,000? The most common answer is between £5,000 and £10,000. The gain has to be disproportionately high to offset the fear of loss.

This insight was sufficiently ground-breaking to earn psychologist Daniel Kahneman a Nobel Prize in Economics[59] and effectively invent what is now known as *behavioural economics.*

Finally, the best way to avoid resistance to change from individuals and groups is not to create it in the first place.

Take a gardening approach and create a shared purpose and shared vision, created by those affected not imposed from above.

You cannot, of course, involve everyone in everything, especially in a big organisation. However, if people see that their viewpoint is represented by others and taken on board, this is the next best thing. Then the number of people on whom you need to practise your empathy skills will be greatly reduced. And never forget that someone who has a reason for opposing a change may have an excellent point.

Exercise

Think about where you sit on the spectrum of fixed to growth mindsets, for something at which you want to be better. Be honest and scale yourself from 0 to 5.

Fixed ◄— Intelligence —► Growth

Avoid Failure ◄— Challenges —► Opportunity to learn

Give up easily ◄— Obstacles —► Persistance

Unecessary if ◄— Effort —► Essential for Mastery
good enough

Get Defensive ◄— Feedback —► Opportunity to learn
and grow

Threat ◄— Others —► Inspiration

Key Points

- Just like a plant, a change needs to be nourished as it grows.
- Attention is one form of nourishment – what are others?
- The roots of culture are assumptions and beliefs, based on our interpretation of experience.
- Group culture is a collectively learned experience.
- In order to change culture, you need to engineer new experiences.
- National culture is something to work with, not to try and change.
- Most have a fixed mindset in at least one aspect of life.
- Fear is one the biggest obstacles to change, but it's normal.
- Empathy is the key to defusing fear.
- Involve those affected to avoid resistance to change.

Enjoy Your Harvest

For a lot of people, there is an intrinsic pleasure in gardening, regardless of the harvest, a bit like sport and the taking part being more important than the winning. But let's be honest, if we grow shrubs for structure that don't grow or flowering plants that don't bloom or bear vegetables and fruit, it's disappointing. And in any event, when it comes to change, we might enjoy the process of learning and growing, but the outcome, the vision, is foremost in our minds.

When I was at primary school, we used to celebrate the *harvest festival*. In the early 1960s in inner London, there weren't yet large supermarkets, with fresh produce from all around the world. So our parents would send us into the school with tins and packets of stuff, alongside commonly available fruit and vegetables. This would be carefully stacked up in the assembly hall and we'd sing songs to celebrate the harvest. I can still remember a Warholesque pyramid of tomato soup cans.

The tradition of celebrating a harvest exists in almost every country in the world. It exists for a reason. It's good to celebrate hard work and enjoy its fruits, and that also applies to personal and organisational change. Therefore, I want to encourage you to look for opportunities to celebrate your successes. If you can, do it with other people in order to multiply the pleasure.

If it's organisational change, ensure you budget includes money for team celebrations. If it's a personal change, celebrate success with a friend or two. Or simply treat yourself to something frivolous. When I got married, my uncle couldn't make the wedding as he was too unwell to travel, but he sent us some money as a present and the card it came in said 'spend it foolishly'.

Don't wait for the final outcome to celebrate. Change can often be difficult. Celebrate significant milestones. It doesn't have to be lavish. Thank those who have helped you along the way. A personal thank you that is meaningful to the recipient will mean a lot more than an anonymous big production.

When we finished the Japanese project that I mentioned earlier, there was a lavish party in Tokyo put on by the client. It was quite some night and was enjoyed by all. After we got back to London, I wanted to do something for our core team – something more personal.

The East End of London, where I grew up, used to have what were known as pie and mash Shops. The pies were a very specific type of meat pie I have never encountered elsewhere. The potato mash was pretty standard, but there was also a parsley sauce, known universally as 'liquor'. Add salt, pepper and vinegar … yes, vinegar … with perhaps some jellied eels alongside and you have a proper East End fast food feast. These shops have all but died out, with only a few remaining.

So I ordered taxis to take the core team, from the City of London, to one of the East End's few remaining pie and mash shops. We crammed into the tiny shop and the adjourned to the pub across the road for pints of Guinness. Whether or not individuals liked the food and drink, they all enjoyed the experience.

The goodwill this generated was off the scale. These were some of the best technicians in the company and, thereafter, if I ever needed help on a project, they were there. If it was someone I hadn't seen for a while, they were likely to say: 'Do you remember that time we went for pie and mash?' And of course I did.

I didn't do it with a quid pro quo in mind. It did it for karma – the joy that comes from saying a thank you that comes from the heart.

Say a thank you that's personal and takes effort.

Conclusion

My biggest concern is that the examples and ideas I have shared in this book have made it sound difficult to think like a gardener. I don't want to leave you with the impression that you need to know that there are nine elements of gardening. And then there is a list of things you should do for each of those elements. That is not my intention. So, I want to leave you with what I think is worth remembering in order of importance.

The core idea to take away from this book is that the organisations you work in and interact with are more like ecosystems than machines. They are unpredictable, so a series of low-risk experiments are more likely to create sustainable change than big-bang, top-down initiatives. If I have convinced you of that and you remember it, then I have achieved my goal in writing this book.

It's a bonus if you also remember that ecosystems are unpredictable because they have many linked elements, some of which are outside of your control. And that can lead to unintended consequences that you should watch out for.

And that really is all you need to know to start thinking like a gardener. After that, the list of elements of gardening is a handy set of prompts that ask you what would pruning, for example, mean in this situation?

The second part of the book contains some ideas and tools that I hope you might find useful, but don't be constrained by them. That said, I'd encourage you to take to heart the messages in the chapter 'Plan'.

Look out for me online at gardenersnotmechanics.com, where I will be sharing more ideas and stories and hoping that you will contribute your own.

Enjoy your gardening!

Appendices

Project Performance Research Summary

In the chapter, 'Machine or Ecosystem?', towards the beginning of the book, I argued that organisational change projects have a poor track record and cited my own research. I also said that there was much rigorous research that supports my argument. The purpose of this appendix is to summarise a sufficient amount of supporting research to make my case. New studies are frequently published, so you may find more up-to-date research. However, it's unlikely that it will arrive at a different conclusion.

All of the research cited below relates to IT projects. That's because the IT industry has been laudably introspective about performance in a way that business change projects have not. Possibly that's because the IT component of a large project is often the most expensive and time-consuming element. Moreover, projects that have a significant IT component are IT-enabled change projects, with other aspects of the project dependent on the IT element. Thus, the performance of IT projects is a good proxy for overall project performance.

The Standish Group Survey of 70,000 Projects

The most-often quoted studies into overruns and their causes come from the Standish Group, whose first report was published in 1995. It was based on replies from 365 respondents, covering 8,380 projects, mainly in the US, and reported that[60]:

- 31% of projects were cancelled before they were completed (being classified as 'impaired');
- 53% cost, on average, 189% of their estimates (being classified as 'challenged');
- Just 16% were delivered on time and on budget (being classified as 'successful').

The report also stated that in large companies, completed projects contained only 42% of their originally proposed features. The figures were better in small companies, with 78% of projects delivering 74% of their originally proposed features. The report concluded that: 'Software development projects are in chaos.' The report was named 'the CHAOS Report' (no-one seems to remember why the word 'chaos' was in upper case, but it has been retained ever since).

Since 1995, the Standish Group has run its survey annually and has developed a subscription service for its data and its advice on best practices, which are derived from that data. By 2010, the CHAOS Report had become the CHAOS Manifesto, with '15 years of data on why projects succeed and fail, representing 70,000 completed IT projects' originating from respondents worldwide. At the time of writing, the latest available figures on 'success and failure' come from projects surveyed in 2008 and reported in 2010. These show that:

- 24% projects were cancelled (either prior to completion or were never used);
- 44% were late, overbudget and/or with less than the required number of features and functions;
- 32% delivered the required features and functions on time and on budget.

As the figures are better than 1996, you might be tempted to conclude that things are slowly improving. Unfortunately, the improvement in performance from 1995 to 2008 masks the fact that the 2008 figures represent what the Standish Group calls 'the highest failure rate in over a decade'.

The Standish Group's interpretation of its data is not without its critics. The January/February 2010 issue of *IEEE Software* magazine[61] features carried an article entitled 'The Rise and Fall of the Chaos Report Figures'. It was written by Professor Chris Verhoef and PhD student J. Laurenz Eveleens, at that time in Vrije Universitiet Amsterdam's Department of Computer Science. Their main criticism seems to relate to the way in which the Standish Group classifies projects as failures or successes. They argue that classifying a project as a failure because it exceeds its budget or schedule is meaningless if the original estimates of cost, schedule and functionality were poor in the first place. They go on to say that:

'The part of a project's success that's related to estimation deviation is highly context dependent. In some contexts 25% estimation error does no harm and doesn't impact what would normally impact project success. In other contexts, only 5% overrun would cause much harm.'

This is all well and good, but it is scant consolation for business managers who have to use cost, schedule and functionality estimates to justify projects in their business cases.

But in any event, the 2010 CHAOS Manifesto only uses the term 'failure' for projects that were cancelled or that delivered something that was never used. Other projects are classified as either 'challenged' or 'successful'. Their classification criteria might have been looser in previous years, but whether a project that exceeds its budget by 25% is a failure or not seems a little academic. The data still says that only a third of projects deliver what was expected on time and on budget.

The other (private) criticism I have heard is that because the Standish Group is selling a service based on its data that advises clients how to achieve better project outcomes, it has a vested interest in painting a dire picture. This begs the question as to whether independent research supports the Standish Group's conclusions. The answer is yes it does, and it comes from the British Computer Society and the Saïd Business School at the University of Oxford.

The British Computer Society

The British Computer Society (BCS) is the UK's professional body for IT. In 2008, it published the results of research that looked at 214 projects, covering the period 1998–2005, across a range of sectors within the EU[62]. The findings are summarised below. An overrun represents a schedule or cost overrun, or both.

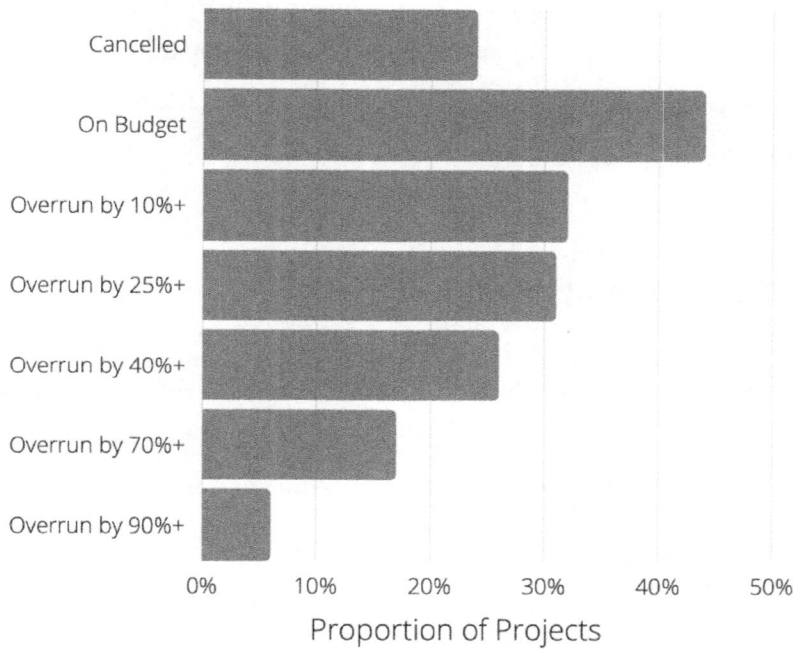

Proportion of Projects

(Note: the overrun bars are cumulative, such that 'overrun by 10%+' includes all of those projects that have overrun by 10% or more, which includes those projects that have overrun by 25%, 40%, 70% and 90%. Similarly, 'overrun by 25%+' includes projects that have overrun by 40%, 70%, 90% and so on for the other bars.)

The figures show that 24% of projects were cancelled after significant expenditure. This is exactly the same figure reported by the Standish

Group. It also shows that 44% of projects were delivered on time and on budget, a better performance than the 32% reported by the Standish Group, though not a million miles away and hardly a cause for celebration.

What really jumped out at me, however, was that 23% of projects of projects overran their budget by 70% or more. Add in the 24% of projects that were cancelled after significant money was spent and pretty close to half of the projects went very badly wrong. This bleak assessment is further supported by the most recent research from the Saïd Business School.

The Saïd Business School

The September 2011 issue of the *Harvard Business Review* published an article entitled 'Why Your IT Project May Be Riskier Than You Think'[63]. It was co-authored by Bent Flyvbjerg, the Professor and Chair of Major Programme Management at the Saïd Business School.

The article reported the initial findings of a study of 1,471 projects worldwide. It found that the average project budget overrun was only 27%, but that: 'Fully one in six of the projects we studied was a black swan, with a cost overrun of 200 per cent, on average, and a schedule overrun of almost 70 per cent.'

This tells us that we should expect most of our IT projects to overrun. Sometimes, however, they will overrun massively. Note that the 200% figure is the magnitude of the overrun, such that a £5 million budget turns into a £15 million cost. You might wonder how a project can become 200% overbudget without someone pulling the plug. Unfortunately, the article doesn't address this question, but in my experience it is a combination of reasons. First and foremost is the belief that so much money has been spent thus far that it would be a waste to 'give up now, with the end in sight'. Unfortunately, the end often remains in sight for a considerable amount of time, but never arrives.

Incidentally, the term 'black swan' comes from Nassim Nicholas Taleb's book *The Black Swan: The Impact of the Highly Improbable*[64]. Taleb describes a black swan as an event that is 'outside the realm of regular expectations … carries an extreme impact … [and is] after the fact explainable and predictable'. This definition will sound very familiar to anyone who has been close to a significant IT project disaster. Here are three (of many) examples:

- British retailer Sainsbury's 'Warehouse Automation' project made it into production in 2003, but was later scrapped in 2005, with a reported write-off of £260 million[65].
- The FBI's 'Virtual Case File' project was written off after an expenditure of $170 million in 2005[66].
- In July 2006, the CEO of Anglo-French Clearing House LCH. Clearnet departed when his company wrote off €47.8 million after scrapping a failed three-year project to build an integrated clearing platform[67].

Can You Defy the Statistics?

Taken together, the studies summarised above tell us that a majority of IT projects overrun, usually by 25% or more, and sometimes when they go wrong, they go very badly wrong. Some people argue that this is simply a question of estimating error. But if your business case depends on the estimate and the project turns out to cost twice as much as you thought it would, then that's pretty serious.

So, do you believe the statistics? If you are like most people, you will fall into one of two camps, depending on whether you are observing someone else's project or whether it is your own project setting out to achieve an important business outcome. The first time I pulled together the data above was for a talk to a class of MBA undergraduates. I had a slide prepared that said something like: 'Only 32% of IT projects deliver what was wanted, on time and budget – one in six overrun by 200% or more.' I was ready to shock them.

'So', I asked them, 'what proportion of IT projects do you think deliver what was expected on time and budget?' I moved to the flip chart to plot the distribution of their answers. 'Zero', someone shouted. I laughed. '5%', shouted another person. My laugh got a bit more nervous, as my presentation storyline evaporated. The final consensus of the 80 or so business students was that no more than 10% of projects deliver what is needed to schedule and budget. When it's not our project, we are very pessimistic about IT projects.

We seem transformed when it is our own project; that innate optimism bias described by Tali Sharot kicks in. Like most car drivers, we believe that accidents will not happen to us because we are better than average drivers. Accidents happen to other people because they are careless and, let's be honest, not as smart as we are. Studies show that people have a problem applying statistical generalisations to themselves. Perversely, however, we tend to generalise based on very few personal experiences, be they good or bad.

So, do you believe you can defy the statistics? Let me throw in one last statistic about project size from the Standish Group research. In its database of 70,000 projects, the Group found that projects with a staff cost of:

- Less than $750,000 have a 71% chance of coming in on time and on budget;
- Between $750,000 and $3 million have a 38% of coming in on time and on budget;
- Over $10 million have a 2% chance of coming in on time and on budget.

This chimes with research that I carried out earlier in my career. I found that the productivity of IT project teams declined exponentially as project size increases. Small is definitely beautiful when it comes to IT projects.

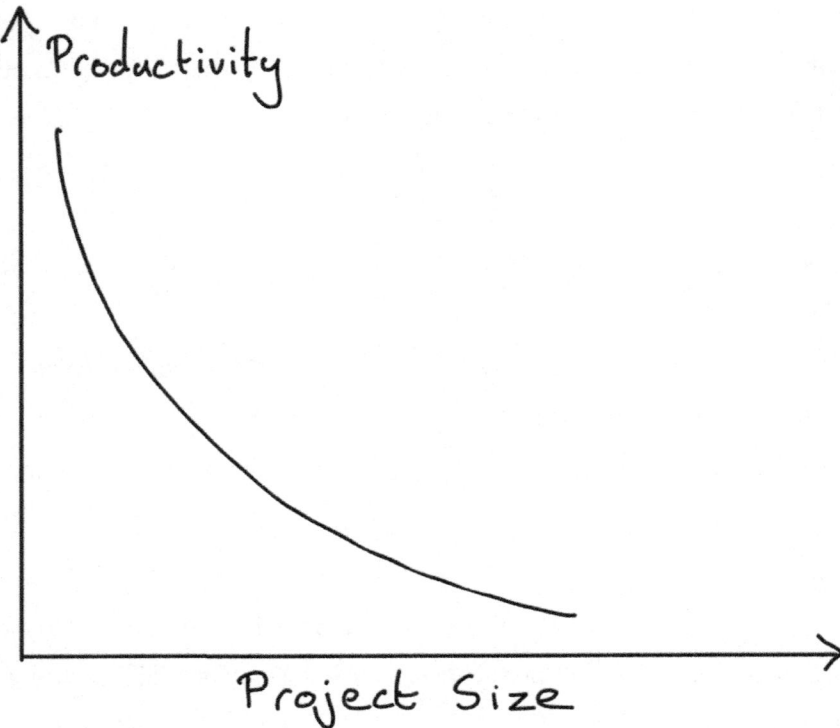

Schedule Approaches

Introduction

I know of three approaches that schedule work in a way that expects circumstances to change as work progresses:

- Scrum
- Kanban
- Last Planner

My aim in this appendix is to give you a thumbnail sketch of each, so that you can explore further if you are interested.

Scrum

Scrum is the best known of the three approaches. It was created and popularised by software developers, although its originators say it was based on product development best practice and codified for software development. In any event, Scrum has now become popular in non-technical disciplines and particularly popular for IT-enabled projects.

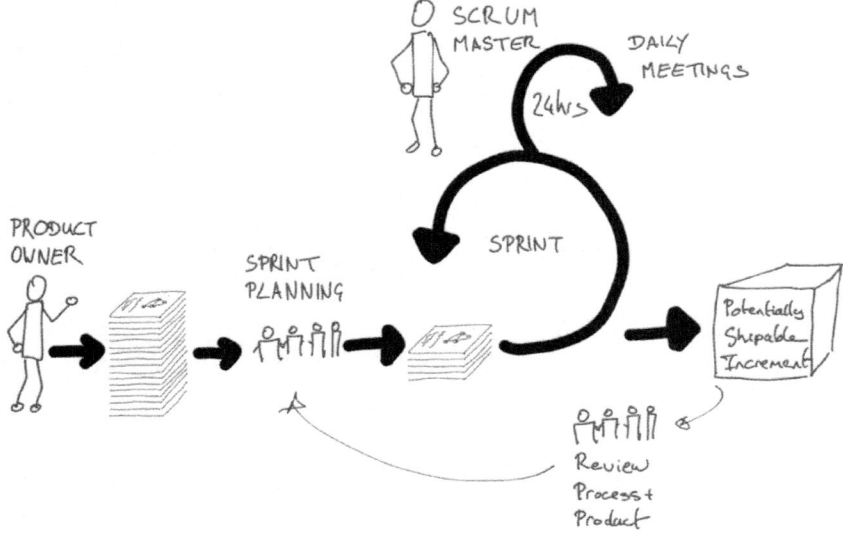

The first step of Scrum is for the product owner to create a list of what they want in the final product. This list is named the product backlog. It is typically composed of one of the following:

- Plain English requirements.
- Features and function.
- User Stories or Use Case (scenario descriptions of what's needed).

The product owner describes each item in 'barely sufficient detail' because it's assumed to be difficult and time-consuming to anticipate and document everything needed in advance. The underlying philosophy of Scrum is iteration and feedback. So, rather than create a pile of documentation, multi-discipline teams work closely together to develop prototypes or versions of what's needed, which converge on the final product.

The second step of Scrum is for the product owner to prioritise the list, such that the development team can work out what can be delivered in a sprint, lasting between one and four weeks. During the sprint, there's a daily 'stand-up' progress review that aims to tackle issues and re-adjust as necessary.

When the development team finish the sprint, the team reviews what's been achieved and decides what will be in the next sprint. Thus, Scrum is a series of sprints, the content of which depends on what happened in the previous sprint and any changing organisational priorities. Each sprint ends with 'potentially shippable product'.

Kanban

Kanban is a scheduling system used in lean manufacturing and was developed by Toyota's Taiichi Ohno. It was adapted for software development by David Anderson[68]. You can use his adaptation for any project, including personal ones such as writing a book.

In manufacturing, the essence of Kanban is that you only manufacture parts when you need them, sometimes known as *just-in-time* manufacturing. Rather than manufacture lots of parts ready for the next step in the process, you only create pieces when the next step requests them.

This demand-led approach is known as *pull*. The purpose of pull is to reduce the amount of *work in progress* because each part waiting to be used represents a cost. Thus, less work in progress equals lower cost.

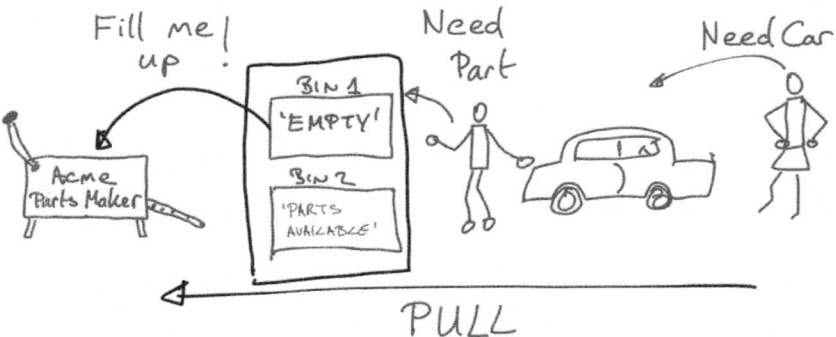

The simplest version of Kanban is that you have three columns drawn on a flip chart or a whiteboard. Each Post-it note represents items of work, preferably of a similar size, such as a week of work:

Then you move the work from left to right so that you can visualise what is complete, what is work in progress and what is waiting.

Proponents of Kanban argue that this *visualisation of the work*, on its own, has a radical cultural impact by encouraging collaboration. Team members congregate around the board, decide what to do next and discuss why some items seem stuck in the 'doing' column. And it's easy to change and adapt to changing circumstances and priorities.

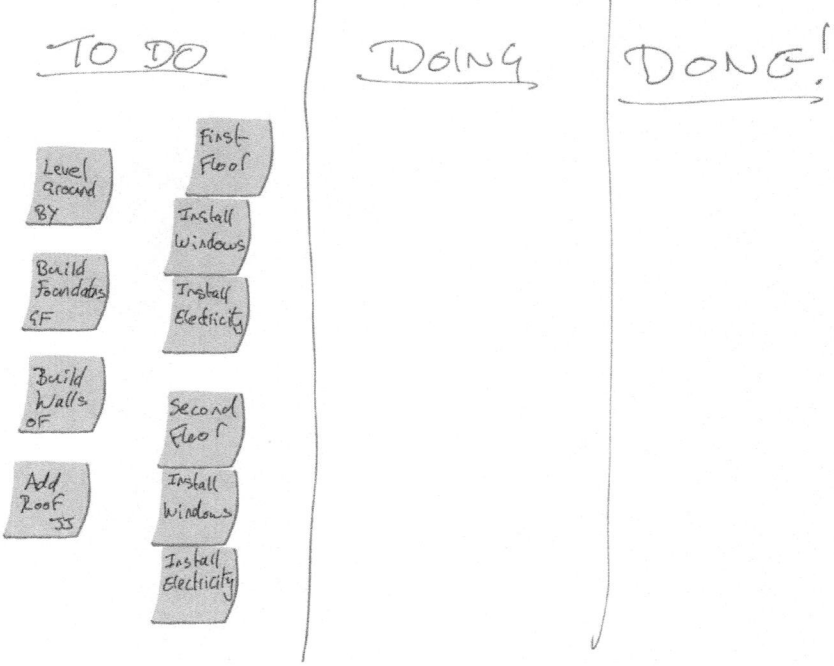

The first refinement of the Kanban approach is to limit the work in progress by reducing the number of items in the 'doing' column. Setting a limit avoids everything being in the 'doing' column because you can only put something new in when something else moves across to the 'done' column.

You can see why this works if you think about your workload. You know that if you work on too many things simultaneously, you never get any of them done because you spread your time too thinly. But what if you set yourself a limit of only working on two things at once? You force yourself to complete work in progress before starting something new.

Alternatively, you can move an item back into the 'to do' column to make space for something else. The same thing thought process happens in teams.

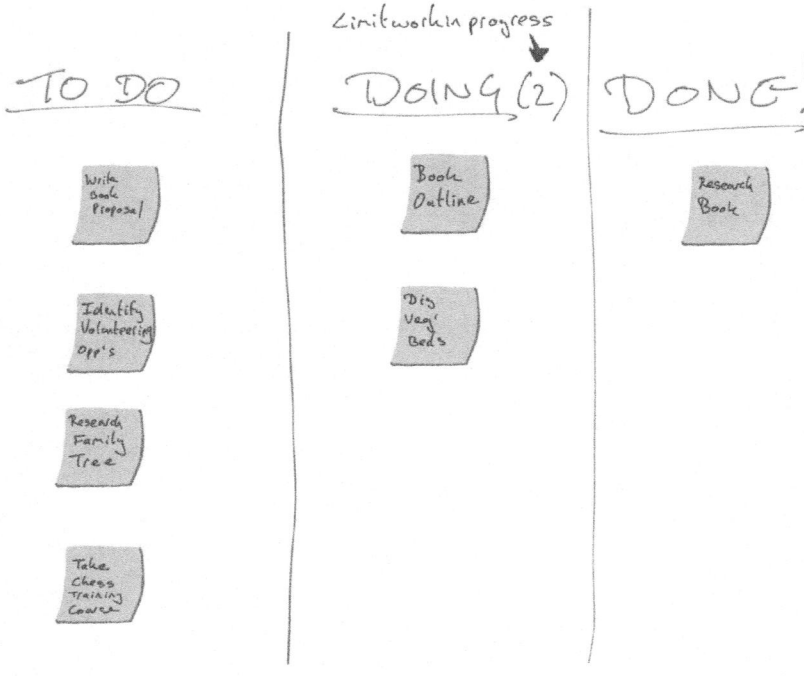

The final refinement is to subdivide the 'doing' column to reflect a repeatable process, such as design-build-test-implement, where each step has its work-in-progress limit.

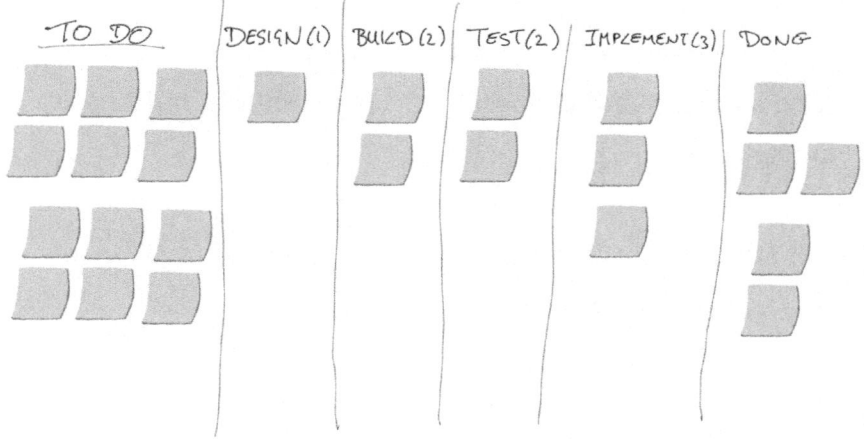

For something like software development, this sets up an interesting dynamic that is similar to the manufacturing origins. I've seen quite a few projects where developers churn out software that piles up in front of the test team that lacks the capacity to deal with it.

However, in a Kanban implementation, the developers can only create software that the test team has the resources to test. The net effect is the need to be balanced in order to ensure a continuous flow of work, thereby saving money by eliminating excess work in progress, just like it did at Toyota.

Last Planner

The *Last Planner System* was created by the *Lean Construction Institute* to apply the principles of lean manufacturing to construction projects. That's because construction projects require the coordination between many different organisations and trades, and this often leads to delays and waste. The Last Planner System therefore has a particularly strong emphasis on collaboration.

But don't think it only applies to construction projects. There are lots of good ideas that can be used in other types of projects where collaboration and waste are concerns. Scheduling usually has three levels of increasing detail:

- A high-level milestone schedule.
- A phase 'pull schedule'.
- A weekly schedule.

A milestone schedule is usually created in response to a request for proposal (RFP). It might be a simple list of dates or it might be a Gantt chart like the one below. Often, a firm will create the milestone schedule before detailed planning, as it assumes past performance is a guide to future performance. Clearly, the higher the degree of novelty, the greater the risk of getting it wrong.

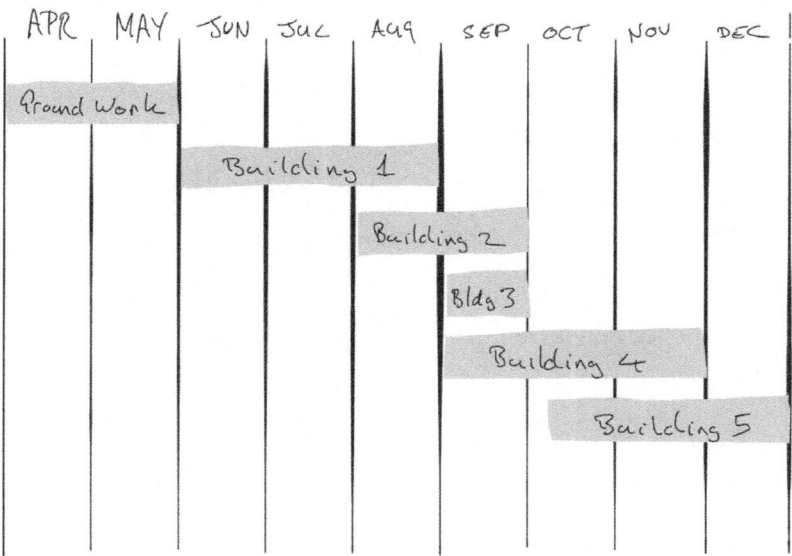

The Last Planner System's detailed scheduling starts with a 'pull schedule'. The Lean Construction Institute recommends that this is done on an extended length of paper, attached to a wall in the site office, with all trades, designers and architects present. The thinking process begins with a milestone that represents an end point, such as the completed construction of a building. A pull schedule typically covers a period of 12–16 weeks.

The facilitator asks three questions:

- What is the last thing that needs to be completed in order to achieve the milestone?
- How long will it take?
- What needs to be completed before it starts (the dependencies)?

The facilitator writes the answers on a Post-it note the colour of which represents the trade responsible for the doing that work, such as concrete, steel, electrical or plumbing.

Then the facilitator asks the same three questions about the dependent tasks until the group has worked backwards through all the work. For this initial pass, there are no dates, only durations.

As the group does this first pass, its members explore together whether durations can be shortened, asking questions like 'would you be able to do it quicker if we…?' Thus, durations are challenged in a supportive way. As teams get more used to this approach, they will often arrive with a set of Post-its for their work rather than figuring it out in the meeting.

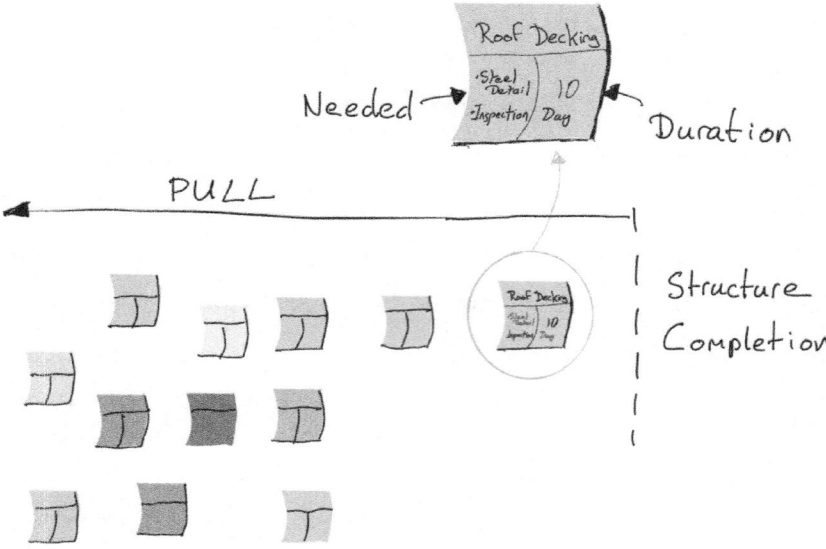

For the next pass, the facilitator adds the timeline, in weeks, working backwards from the milestone date. If this reveals mismatches compared to the RFP response, the group discusses how these mismatches can be resolved. It's at this stage that annotations are added where helpful.

For example, a project might require a particularly big lifting crane that needs to be hired and is only available within a short timeframe. The teams have to work around this and it's worth highlighting it on the schedule. The identification of constraints is an essential part of the scheduling process, and these are noted on a separate list.

At the end of the scheduling process, photographs are taken of the final schedule and distributed across the site.

The next step in the Last Planner System is to create a week plan for the coming week. It's a more detailed version of the pull schedule for the week in question and is created collaboratively at the beginning of each week. The column at the end is for 'percentage of plan complete' (PPC). measured by the proportion of Post-its that get completed, in order to alert the group to knock-on effects.

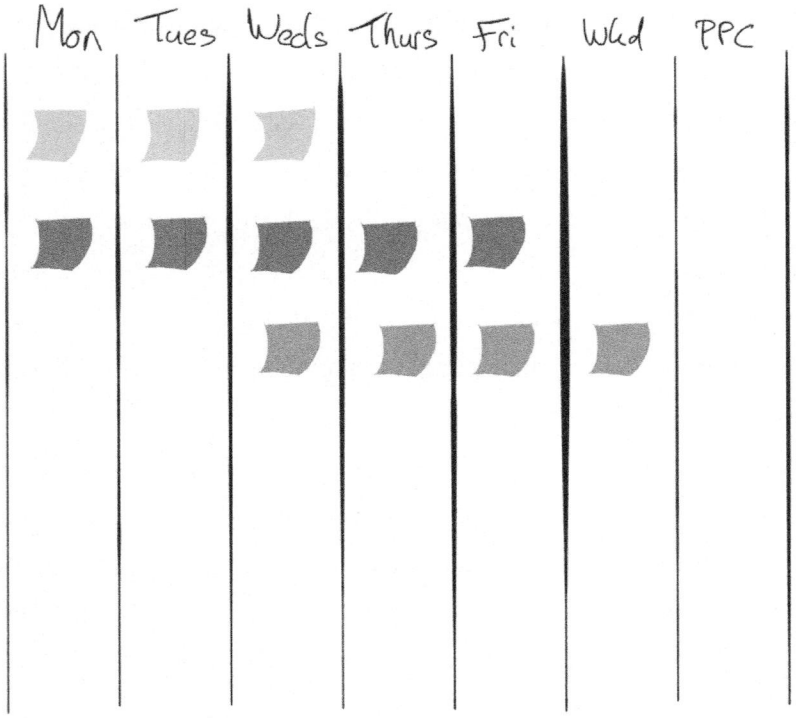

the teams create the weekly plan, they do a 'six-week look ahead'. This does not, as you might imagine, involve reviewing what is coming up in the next six weeks. The purpose is to look at the specific week that is six weeks in the future and look backwards, to ensure that all of the teams know what they need to have ready by that time. It assumes that most construction delays can be resolved within a six-week timeframe.

The Last Planner System is so-called because the people who do the work are the ones who create and maintain the schedule. And it's deliberately done in a simple way that is easy to change, without the need for any computer skills.

A subtlety that might not be immediately obvious is that pull scheduling reduces a lot of waste. It avoids the creation of stuff in anticipation of a need.

This sort of waste doesn't just occur in construction projects. I have seen quite a few joint-venture start-ups in which project teams churned out tons of documentation, such as procedures, that were never used by the operational teams who inherited them.

Similarly, I've seen lots of detailed software development documentation produced for things that were never built.

Summary

I hope I have remained neutral when describing each of the three scheduling approaches. Different ones suit different needs and preferences, so I don't want to say that one is better than the other. However, I think each approach has its strengths and weaknesses, such that hybrid approaches may yield the best results.

My advice is to avoid dogma. Each of the three approaches has a management consultancy industry that has grown up around it. And to differentiate themselves, you may find many of those firms telling you that there is one best way, with lots of *standards*, so you need their help to do it right!

I say keep it simple and experiment: use a simple version of one of them to collaboratively visualise the work, using Post-it notes on a wall, in a shared space.

If one of the three approaches attracts you, have a look at my *Gardeners not Mechanics* YouTube channel, where there's a playlist named *scheduling*[69]. It's much easier to understand each of them if you see them in action. Describing them on the page doesn't bring them to life in the way that a demonstration can.

On the playlist, there's a talk that Ken Schwaber, one of Scrum's originators, did at Google. It's a great description of the essence of Scrum, without the fluff.

Similarly, there are four videos from Jason Mayes, the Chairman of the Lean Construction Institute, in which he shows you how it is done.

I couldn't find anything as good for Kanban, so I have included some stuff I did myself for my Lean Project Management course. You could also do a lot worse than read David Anderson's relatively short book *Kanban*, in which you can read about the essence without the pedantic stuff that has been accumulating since.

I've also included a few other things that you might find useful.

51 Mental Formations

These are the 51 Mental Formations that Thich Nhat Hanh had to learn as a 16-year-old novice monk in Vietnam. As you'll see, he added some more of his own as he journeyed towards becoming a Zen Master. I've included them here to illustrate the reference I made to them in the chapter, 'Water'. It is beyond the scope of this book to offer explanations of all of the terms below, but if you'd like to know about Buddhist thought, the Plum Village app is a great place to start, with lots of recording of talk by Thich Nhat Hanh. Alternatively, there's the Plum Village channel on YouTube.

5 Universals	5 Particulars
Contact	Intention
Attention	Determination
Feeling	Mindfulness
Perception	Concentration
Volition	Insight

11 Wholesome	Plus Those Added by Thich Nhat Hanh
Faith	Non-fear
Inner Shame	Absence of Anxiety
Shame before Others	Stability, Solidity
Absence of Craving	Loving Kindness
Absence of Hatred	Compassion
Absence of Ignorance	Joy
Diligence, Energy	Humility
Tranquillity, Ease	Happiness
Vigilance, Energy	Feverlessness
Equanimity	Freedom/Sovereignty
Non-harming	

6 Primary Unwholesome	
Craving, Covetous	Hatred
Ignorance, Confusion	Arrogance

Doubt, Suspicion	Wrong View

20 Secondary Unwholesome	
10 Minor Secondary Unwholesome	*2 Middle Secondary Unwholesome*
Anger	Lack Inner Shame
Resentment, Enmity	Lack of Shame before Others
Concealment	
Maliciousness	*8 Greater Secondary Unwholesome*
Jealousy	Restlessness
Selfishness, Parsimony	Drowsiness
Deceitfulness, Fraud	Lack of Faith, Unbelief
Guile	Laziness
Desire to Harm	Negligence
Pride	Forgetfulness
	Distraction
	Lack of Discernment
Plus Those Added by Thich Nhat Hanh	
Fear	Anxiety
Despair	

4 Indeterminate	
Regret, Repentance	Sleepiness
Initial Thought	Sustained Thought

References

[1] Graham-Harrison, Emma. 'Propaganda and Sexism Prove Powerful Contraceptives for Chinese Women', The Guardian, 17 January 2020, https://www.theguardian.com/world/2020/jan/17/propaganda-and-sexism-prove-powerful-contraceptives-for-chinese-women

[2] Fong, Mei. *One Child: The Story of China's Most Radical Experiment.* Boston New York: Houghton Mifflin Harcourt USA, 2016.

[3] 'The Disrupters, Mumsnet: Justine Roberts', *BBC Radio 4*, 4 December 2018, https://www.bbc.co.uk/programmes/p06tngnc.

[4] London School of Economics and Political Science. 'Radical Uncertainty: Decision Making for an Unknowable Future', https://www.lse.ac.uk/lse-player?facet=all&term=radical%20uncertainty.

[5] King, Mervyn, and John Kay. *Radical Uncertainty: Decision-Making for an Unknowable Future.* Bridge Street Press, 2020.

[6] Lloyd, Christopher. 'Elements of Gardening', *The Guardian*, 15 February 2003, https://www.theguardian.com/lifeandstyle/2003/feb/15/shopping.gardens.

[7] HBR Store. 'Ron Johnson: A Career in Retail ^ 516016'. Accessed 2 April 2020. https://store.hbr.org/product/ron-johnson-a-career-in-retail/516016.

[8] 'The Right Way to Solve Complex Business Problems'. *Harvard Business Review*, 4 December 2018, https://hbr.org/podcast/2018/12/the-right-way-to-solve-complex-business-problems.

[9] Duprey, Rich. 'Maybe Ron Johnson was Right about J.C. Penney After All'. *The Motley Fool*, 18 January 2019, https://www.fool.com/investing/2019/01/18/maybe-ron-johnson-was-right-about-jc-penney-after.aspx.

[10] 'Rolling Thunder Revue: A Bob Dylan Story by Martin Scorsese (2019)', *IMDb*, https://www.imdb.com/title/tt9577852/mediaviewer/rm3833030400 (accessed 2 April 2020).

[11] Lloyd, Gary. 'Change Needs Gardeners Not Mechanics'. *ITNOW* 58(2) (1 June 2016): 54–55, https://doi.org/10.1093/itnow/bww052.

[12] Hammer, Michael, and Jim Champy. *Reengineering the Corporation: A Manifesto for Business Revolution*. Reprint with corrections edition. Allen & Unwin, 1993.

[13] Kotter, John P. 'Leading Change: Why Transformation Efforts Fail'. Harvard Business Review, 1 May 1995, https://hbr.org/1995/05/leading-change-why-transformation-efforts-fail-2
[14] Kotter, John P. *Leading Change*. Harvard Business Review Press, 1995

[15] Kotter, John P. 'Accelerate!' *Harvard Business Review*, 1 November 2012, https://hbr.org/2012/11/accelerate.

[16] Kahneman, Daniel, Andrew M. Rosenfield, Linnea Gandhi and Tom Blaser. 'Noise: How to Overcome the High, Hidden Cost of Inconsistent Decision Making', *Harvard Business Review*, 1 October 2016, https://hbr.org/2016/10/noise.

[17] De Gruyter. 'Diagnosis', https://www.degruyter.com/view/journals/dx/dx-overview.xml (accessed 2 April 2020).

[18] '"Nobody Took Charge" in Rail Timetable Chaos', *BBC News*, 20 September 2018, https://www.bbc.com/news/business-45572736.

[19] 'The Trouble with England's Test and Trace System – Podcast'. *The Guardian*, 20 August 2020, presented by Rachel Humphreys with Josh Halliday; produced by Hannah, Axel Kacoutié; executive producers Phil

Maynard and Nicole Jackson,
https://www.theguardian.com/news/audio/2020/aug/20/the-trouble-with-englands-test-and-trace-system-podcast.

[20] Covey, Stephen R. *The 7 Habits of Highly Effective People: 30th Anniversary Edition*. Simon & Schuster USA, 2020.

[21] BBC. 'BBC Radio 4 - Desert Island Discs, Tom Hanks'. Accessed 7 December 2020. https://www.bbc.co.uk/programmes/b079m78n.

[22] Ries, Eric. *The Lean Startup*. New York: Crown Publishing Group, 2011.

[23] Isaacs, Kate, and Deborah Ancona. '3 Ways to Build a Culture of Collaborative Innovation'. *Harvard Business Review*, 12 August 2019, https://hbr.org/2019/08/3-ways-to-build-a-culture-of-collaborative-innovation.

[24] Roos, Daniel, Massachusetts Institute of Technology and James P. Womack. *Machine That Changed the World: The Massachusetts Institute of Technology 5-Million-Dollar, 5-Year Report on the Future of the Automobile Industry*. Scribner, 1990.

[25] Deming, W. Edwards. *Out of the Crisis*. MIT Center for Advanced Engineering Study, 1986.

[26] Defeo, Joseph. *Juran's Quality Essentials*. McGraw-Hill Education, 2014.

[27] Gary Lloyd. *Cummings Why Leave Won the Referendum*, 2020. https://www.youtube.com/watch?v=LR8SgalQCGM&feature=youtu.be.

[28] The Guardian. 'What Is No 10's "moonshot" Covid Testing Plan and Is It Feasible?', 9 September 2020. http://www.theguardian.com/world/2020/sep/09/what-is-no-10s-moonshot-covid-testing-plan-and-is-it-feasible.

[29] 'Are You Solving the Right Problems?', *HBR Store*, 1 January 2017, https://store.hbr.org/product/are-you-solving-the-right-problems/R1701D.

[30] 'Former Apple Employee Recounts How Jobs Motivated IPhone Team', *Engadget*, 4 February 2012, https://www.engadget.com/2012-02-04-former-apple-employee-recounts-how-jobs-motivated-iphone-team.html.

[31] Gary Lloyd. *Microsoft CEO Ballmer Laughs at IPhone*, 2020. https://www.youtube.com/watch?v=oQgABtTWQtg&feature=youtu.be.

[32] Gary Lloyd. *Designed by Apple in California*, 2020. https://www.youtube.com/watch?v=89dwxM5UYmo&feature=youtu.be.

[33] Kotler, Philip T., and Gary Armstrong. *Principles of Marketing*, 17th edn. Pearson, 2017.

[34] Walker, Amy. 'HS2's Northern Critics: "We Don't Need it But We'll Be Paying for it"', *The Guardian*, 4 February 2020, https://www.theguardian.com/uk-news/2020/feb/04/hs2s-northern-critics-we-dont-need-it-but-well-be-paying-for-it.

[35] Sutherland, Rory. *Alchemy: The Surprising Power of Ideas That Don't Make Sense*. WH Allen, 2019.

[36] Senge, Peter M. *The Fifth Discipline, the Art & Practice of the Learning Organization*. Doubleday Currency, 1990.

[37] Hughes, Daniel. Moltke on the Art of War. Novato, California: Presidio, 1993

[38] 'What Technique Does the Military Use to Make Sure Plans Work on the Battlefield?', *Barking up the Wrong Tree*, 14 November 2012, https://www.bakadesuyo.com/2012/11/technique-military-plans-work-battlefield.

[39] 'In Search Of Excellence: Lessons from America's Best-Run Companies' Robert H Waterman Jr, Peters, Tom, Peters & Water. 2nd (Second) Edition on 15 April 2004, n.d.

[40] Ries, Eric. *The Lean Startup*. New York: Crown Publishing Group, 2011.

[41] Gary Lloyd. *Zen Master Thich Nhat Hanh on SelectiveWatering*, 2020. https://www.youtube.com/watch?v=khtkQ-l2swo&feature=youtu.be.

[42] Barrett, Lisa Feldman. *How Emotions are Made: The Secret Life of the Brain*. Macmillan, 2017.

[43] Ross, Elizabeth Kubler. *On Death and Dying: What the Dying Have to Teach Doctors, Nurses, Clergy and Their Own Families*. Simon & Schuster, 2003.

[44] Kessler, Elisabeth, and David Kubler-Ross. *On Grief and Grieving: Finding the Meaning of Grief through the Five Stages of Loss*. Simon & Schuster UK, 2014.

[45] 'FORDEC', *AviationKnowledge*, http://aviationknowledge.wikidot.com/aviation:fordec. 'Sony Global – Product & Technology Milestones – Personal Audio',

[46] Morgan, Adam, and Mark Barden. *A Beautiful Constraint: How to Transform Your Limitations into Advantages, and Why it's Everyone's Business*. John Wiley & Sons, 2015.

[47] https://www.sony.net/SonyInfo/CorporateInfo/History/sonyhistory-e.html.

[48] Schein, Edgar H. *Organizational Culture and Leadership*, 5th edition. Wiley, 2016.

[49] Gray, Dave, and Richard Saul Wurman. *Liminal Thinking: Create the Change You Want by Changing the Way You Think*. Rosenfeld Media, 2016.

[50] Meyer, Erin. *Culture Map*. PublicAffairs, 2016.

[51] Gelfand, Michele. *Rule Makers, Rule Breakers: How Tight and Loose Cultures Wire Our World*. Scribner Book Company, 2018.

[52] Dweck, Carol. *Mindset: How You Can Fulfil Your Potential*. Robinson, 2012.

[53] Plomin, Robert. *Blueprint: How DNA Makes Us Who We are.* MIT Press, 2018.

[54] London School of Economics and Political Science. 'Nature vs Nurture', https://www.lse.ac.uk/Events/LSE-Festival/Shape-The-World/Events/20200307/nature-nurture.aspx.

[55] Eagleman, David. *Livewired: The Inside Story of the Ever-Changing Brain.*Canongate Books, 2020.

[56] Cialdini, Robert B. *Influence: The Psychology of Persuasion.* HarperCollins, 1984.

[57] 'The Scientists Persuading Terrorists to Spill Their Secrets', *The Guardian*, 13 October 2017, https://www.theguardian.com/news/2017/oct/13/the-scientists-persuading-terrorists-to-spill-their-secrets.

[58] Voss, Chris. *Never Split the Difference: Negotiating as if Your Life Depended on it.* HarperCollins USA, 2016.

[59] Kahneman, Daniel, and Amos Tversky. 'Prospect Theory: An Analysis of Decision under Risk'. *Econometrica* 47(2) (1979): 263–291 https://doi.org/10.2307/1914185

[60] The Standish Group, https://www.standishgroup.com.

[61] Eveleens, J. Laurenz, and Chris Verhoef. 'The Rise and Fall of the Chaos Report Figures', *IEEE Software* 27(1) (January 2010): 30–36, https://doi.org/10.1109/MS.2009.154.

[62] McManus, John, and Trevor Wood-Harper. 'A Study in Project Failure', *BCS - The Chartered Institute for IT*, https://www.bcs.org/content-hub/a-study-in-project-failure.

[63] 'Why Your IT Project May Be Riskier Than You Think', *HBR Store.* 1 September 2011, https://store.hbr.org/product/why-your-it-project-may-be-riskier-than-you-think/F1109A.

[64] Taleb, Nassim Nicholas. *The Black Swan: Second Edition: The Impact of the Highly Improbable: With a New Section: 'On Robustness and Fragility'.* Random House, 2007.

[65] 'Sainsburys Dogged by Supply Chain Problems', *Information Age*. 10 February 2006, https://www.information-age.com/sainsburys-dogged-by-supply-chain-problems-292891.

[66] 'Who Killed the Virtual Case File?', *IEEE Spectrum: Technology, Engineering, and Science News*, 1 September 2005, https://spectrum.ieee.org/computing/software/who-killed-the-virtual-case-file.

[67] 'New Management at LCH. Clearnet Writes Off Failed IT Project as Cost Rises to €67.9 Million', *Global Custodian*, 21 July 2006, https://www.globalcustodian.com/new-management-at-lch-clearnet-writes-off-failed-it-project-as-cost-rises-to-amp836467-9-million.

[68] Anderson, David J. *Kanban*. Blue Hole Press Inc., 2013.

[69] 'Scheduling', *YouTube*, https://www.youtube.com/playlist?list=PLEenuZxWutZJK8kJS0-tafYGjzObCQ3T1.

Index

245

Printed in Great Britain
by Amazon

28859017R00145